What people sa
Nick James

"If you want your own online
the guy that's been doing it for over a decade with ᴏᴜ ...
Success! That would be my friend Nick James! And the best place to start
is by reading this book!"

Bill Glazer
Best-Seller Author, Professional Speaker,
Copywriter,

"Nick's marketing methods are truly inspirational. You can't go far
wrong if you stick to these principles and strategies, which is exactly why I
believe you should read this book from cover to cover."

Clate Mask
Keap.com (formerly known as InfusionSoft.com)

"Nick James is a true inspiration to every business owner or budding
new entrepreneur. It's no surprise that recently Nick won 'Internet Marketer
Of The Year' as voted for by over 200 other business leaders and full-time
marketers.

Matt Bacak,
MattBacak.com

"Nick gets straight to the point, providing the exact steps he takes in his
own business, showing the way to make an additional six figures per year."

Laura Casselman
CEO, JVZoo.com

If you would like to share your thoughts and feedback
about this book or any of our other products and services, we
invite you to leave your own comments online at:
www.MyCustomerComments.com

Secrets Of Six-Figure Earners

Building a $100,000+ Business in Info Publishing

Nick James

Acknowledgements

In previous acknowledgements I have focussed my thanks on those I have personally learned from. This time however my thanks are focussed squarely on you, our customer.

Thank you for investing in the information products we create. Without you we would not exist.

Thank you also to the 12 customers featured in this book. Without them this book would not exist.

It is my hope that you will be inspired by each case study and that we may, in the future be able to feature your accomplishments in the next volume of this *'Secrets of Six Figure Earners'* book series.

To be considered for the next book, please reach out to us with details about your business journey so far via email at: admin@nickjamesadmin.com.

It's worth noting that there is 'a special transformation' that takes place when action is regularly added to knowledge. If you'd like some help to make that happen, be sure to follow the instructions at the end of this book inviting you to take your next steps with me.

Finally, I'd also like to thank Rob Cuesta at Bright Flame Books for his help and encouragement in creating, editing and publishing this book.

About the Author

Nick James has built 3 separate million dollar a year internet businesses since his entrepreneurial journey began in 2001.

Nick is a true example of a self-made success and it's his own personal experience that makes him understanding and approachable on all business levels, working with enthusiastic entrepreneurs at varying stages of their journey into business.

Business coach, mentor, software developer, internet marketing expert – Nick James won *'Internet Marketer Of The Year'* 2016-2017 and won *'Outrageous Marketer Of The Year'* in 2020.

Websites:

www.Nick-James.com
www.SixFiguresAYear.com
www.SeriousAboutSixFigures.com

Contents

Why This Book? Why Now?

This is a book about building an "information publishing" business. So, before we go much further, it would make sense to make sure we are all clear on what that phrase means.

Most people associate the word "publishing" with books. However, info publishing is much more than that. It's about getting your information out into the world in whatever format you want. Some people record themselves on camera; others record audio or write a special report. Some interview other people and turn that into a course, a product, a podcast, regular newsletters, or whatever works for their audience. And, as you'll see in a couple of the chapters, you can even turn it into a book if that's the direction you want to go - but it's your choice.

There are no limits and no expectations in this industry. You simply do whatever works for you and your audience. And in this book, you will meet people who have each interpreted info publishing in their own slightly different way.

Much more important than the specific format is the idea of creating what I call a "product staircase": as you read about different people's businesses, you'll notice that they don't just have one single offer. Instead, they have several things to sell at different price points, from a few dollars to thousands of dollars, and most of them offer a way for clients to work with them directly through individual or group coaching, a mastermind group, or something similar.

Too often, I hear people making excuses for why they can't start a business and why they won't be successful. They'll look at an info publisher who's absolutely crushing it and say, "It's alright for them, they're still young. It's too late for me to start a business," or - just as often - "I can't start my business yet. I'm too young and inexperienced." Or perhaps they'll say, "I can't start a business. I don't have any money." Or "It's alright for that person. They work in X niche. But all I know is Z." Or "It's alright for that person. They had a list/X background/connections/experience/whatever. I don't have that. Poor me."

The info publishers you'll read about in this book all come from very different backgrounds. Some, like Mark Walker, come from a corporate environment; others, like Amber Jalink, start a business to supplement their family income. Some, like Raj Sidhu, start their business right at the beginning of their working life; others, like Fred Ray Lybrand, do it to stay active in retirement (and create a very comfortable retirement, of course!). So, whatever stage you are at in life, and whatever your reason for becoming an info publisher, I hope you will find at least one person in this book - preferably more - whose story resonates with you.

You'll also find that there is no secret niche that guarantees success. The info publishers in this book have built businesses in all sorts of topics, from creating blank journals to locksmithing. So, whatever your area of expertise, you can create a product to teach people and start selling it. And as you'll read in the book, it really doesn't take long to set up a site and start driving traffic.

Finally, every business owner in this book had to overcome some form of adversity on their way to success. No one started a business and became an overnight sensation - in fact, most of the people you read about failed at least once. And they all started from different places financially: some had redundancy payouts, second incomes, or other funds behind them, while others didn't have two pennies to rub together when they set up their info publishing company.

What every person you read about does have in common is this: when the opportunity appeared, they said "Yes," and embraced it. They also share two other characteristics: they are all customers of mine, and they have achieved extraordinary success in their info-publishing business (not only financially but also by their own definition of what success means).

The one story that's missing in this book is mine. The reason for that is simple. I've already told that story in my earlier book, Six Figures a Year in Info Publishing (and if you haven't got a copy, you can get it free at www.SixFiguresAYear.com). So, in this book, I decided to focus on the stories of ordinary people just like you who have achieved success - by the definition they chose - in info publishing.

It would have been easy to give you the impression that everything in growing your info publishing business is always wonderful. I could have picked the case studies very carefully and told them to only talk about the positives and leave out anything negative that had happened along their way.

I could have, but I didn't.

Why? Because that doesn't help you. And ultimately, it doesn't help me.

When you become an info publisher, I want you to make that decision with as much information in your hands as possible. I want you to know what to expect - the good and the bad. I want you to know that every business owner goes through rough patches; times when you'll look at your business and wonder if it's ever going to be a success; when you'll question whether you made the right decision.

But I also want you to know that there is support available through all those difficulties and that on the other side of the struggle, there is a rewarding, fulfilling career that you control. You decide how much work you put into it and how much reward you need to get out of it.

CHAPTER 1

Amber Jalink

A question I often hear from business owners is, "What should I sell?" (Or, if they've been in business for a while, "What should I sell <u>next</u>?") If you're lucky, your customers will tell you exactly what they want. That's how Amber Jalink came up with the idea for *The Journal Creator*.

Amber, from Niagara Falls, Canada, had grown a business selling journal templates as a sideline to her main info publishing business. Some of her buyers started asking if she also sold software to create journals, and when she said she didn't, most of them replied, "Please, build it!" So, she did.

There's an important lesson here: if enough of your customers tell you they want something, listen. And if it's something you want to offer, go for it.

Many info publishers would outsource software creation to a programmer. However, Amber had done that in the past and didn't want to go down that path again. So, even though she isn't a programmer, she decided to figure it out for herself.

Most people would find the idea of coding scary, but it needn't be. Today there are many "No-code" development platforms that make it easy to write software yourself: if you can draw a flowchart and build a basic HTML website, you probably have enough technical know-how to create a working software tool that you can sell!

> *Even if you outsource work, you should still learn how to do it yourself. Because if you don't understand the basics of what people are doing for you, it's too easy to lose money.* **Amber Jalink**

Today, The Journal Creator has 400 customers, with 50 of them paying an additional monthly subscription for access to extra templates and features. Not bad for a side business built around software Amber wrote herself (without expensive coders or designers) - and it's not even her main business!

How It All Started

Amber has been online since the early days of the internet, back in 1997. She had worked as an executive secretary and ended up teaching Microsoft Office. However, like many people who leave the corporate world to become online entrepreneurs, she was sick of office politics. So, when her husband, Aaron, got a new job in western Canada, it gave her the perfect out.

For a while, as the couple settled into their new environment, Amber wasn't working. Then kids came along, and she stayed home to look after them. Finally, just as she was planning to re-enter the corporate world, the Universe threw her a curveball. Their son got sick, and because of his condition, he couldn't go to daycare. Someone had to stay home to look after him, and that someone was Amber.

Her husband's salary was enough to cover the bills and their living expenses, but there was nothing left over. Eventually, the pressure for Amber to start earning again began to build. They wanted a new car, and they were looking forward to buying their own home and moving out of their rental - but they couldn't do that on a single income. So, they paid a friend to babysit, and Amber went out to work.

Problem solved - or so you'd think. But with only one car in the family, Amber had to drop Aaron at work, drive across town to her job, then cross town again at the end of the day to pick him up. And even though Amber had always been a home cook, after a long day at work and the double commute, it was easier to get takeout on the way. In the end, even though Amber had a good salary, the cost of all the takeouts and the extra babysitting added up to more than she made after tax. Financially, it didn't make sense.

And then there was their son's illness. He had good days and bad days, but even on a good day, his condition could change in minutes. Amber realized she needed the kind of flexibility a corporate job could never give her. So, she called it a day and handed in her notice.

Spending more time at home with the family is a common reason for becoming an info publisher - even when you don't have a sick kid.

Getting Online

Today, it's easier than ever to start an online business, but things were very different in the 1990s. Back then, most people hadn't even heard of the internet, and Newsweek was still calling it a passing fad that would never catch on!

Amber's entry into the world of online business was, in her own words, "crazy." Aaron worked in IT and had been a beta tester when Microsoft introduced the Microsoft Network, so she'd had a little exposure to the online world. The couple paid $20 a month for an internet connection at home, and Amber started hunting. She bought an income opportunities magazine and wrote *letters* (this was 1997, remember, and most people still didn't have email) to ten of the advertisers offering to do secretarial work from home - long before "working from home" was even a thing!

A week passed. Crickets. Then another week. Still nothing.

It was a nail-biting six weeks before the phone rang. It was someone from one of the businesses Amber had written to, but instead of a secretarial position, the caller asked if she wanted to sell grant packets through newspaper and radio ads. That meant spending money Amber didn't have, so she asked if she could sell them online instead. At the time, the internet was still new and unknown, so he was skeptical. He told her she could try but not to get her hopes up.

That month, Amber made her first $100, which turned into $12,000 by the end of the first year: not bad in a world where online business was still almost unheard of, and if you wanted to browse a website, you had to disconnect your phone from the wall, plug in a dial-up modem, and wait a few minutes while everything connected!

Growing The Business

One of the big ideas that fired Amber's imagination was building a marketing list, sending them an email newsletter, and charging companies for ad space in the newsletter.

Initially, the subscriber list grew slowly. But then she connected with other newsletter owners, and they started doing ad swaps - where two businesses promote each other to their own list. That's when things started to take off

As the newsletter grew in popularity, more and more people approached Amber to ask if they could write articles for it. In the end, the newsletter got so long that Amber worried people would stop reading it. But then inspiration struck again, and she started putting the articles on a separate website to create one of the first online marketing ezines. She would email a daily summary of the new articles published on the site that day and let the customer pick which ones they wanted to read.

That created a new opportunity: as well as selling ad spots in the email newsletter, Amber could also sell space on the website and double her revenue.

Then Google launched AdSense: website owners could sell adverting space to Google, who would feed ads to it and give the site owner a share of the ad revenue. As the site grew in popularity, so did Amber's income, both from AdSense and from individual advertisers.

That became Amber's business model for the next ten years, and revenue grew every year. Like any business, however, it wasn't all plain sailing. Sales in the second year reached $72,000 - a 6x increase. But in 2000, Aaron lost his job, and the family moved back across the country to Ontario. Then, just as the family was settling back in, the unimaginable happened: their son died.

Dealing With Challenges

From that point on, every day became a struggle. Amber stepped back from actively promoting the business to focus on supporting her husband and their surviving daughter as they dealt with what was going on. And that's a major benefit of running an info publishing business: it carried on ticking over without her until she was ready to come back to it. The ad revenue from the newsletter kept the family going that year.

With life throwing so many challenges her way, it would have been easy in the early days for Amber to decide she'd made a mistake and give up. The pivotal moment came while the family was still dealing with the loss of Aaron's job and the death of their son.

The couple had been driving Amber's father's beaten-up old Buick, which was on its last legs. He had given them the car when they moved back to Ontario because they'd had to leave their own cars out west, and they needed something to get around.

The car was due for an emissions test which the couple knew the old Buick would never pass. So, they headed to a dealership owned by a family friend and found a car for $10,000 - nothing fancy but good enough to get around - and they asked about financing.

Their friend looked over their accounts and shook his head. Financially, the previous twelve months had been brutal: Aaron had lost his job, and Amber's focus had been on the family, not her business. So, even though they didn't have any existing debt, he told them they wouldn't be able to get a loan.

Amber and Aaron tried arguing that they had money coming in. But their friend wouldn't listen. He didn't care how much money was going to come in in the future. All that counted was what was on their last tax return, which wasn't great (a situation many business owners can relate to).

One "Small" Detail

On their way out, Aaron pointed to their friend's car and asked, "How much do those go for?"

The dealer laughed. "You couldn't afford it."

The couple hadn't told him everything, however. Yes, the last twelve months had been tough. But Amber had been keeping her mind busy so she wouldn't dwell on everything that had happened.

She'd started getting ideas, and when she finally got back into the right headspace to pick up the business, she had created one of the first ad networks, charging to connect advertisers to other publishers who wanted to sell ad space. And even though it was a lifestyle business designed to give Amber the flexibility to spend time with her family, it was bringing in more money than most people in very senior full-time jobs were earning.

In fact, the business was on track to make $200,000 in sales that year (around $300,000 in Canadian dollars at the time). As a result, Amber and Aaron were in a position to pay the full price of the car in cash - they had only asked about a loan because they were still being careful about managing their cash flow.

Two weeks later, they walked into the Lexus dealership in town and bought a brand-new car, paid in full, with no financing. That was when Amber knew things were getting back on track and the business was real. It wasn't just about paying the bills anymore: her hard work also allowed them to enjoy a lifestyle.

There will be people - family and friends - who tell you, "Go get a real job." Ignore them. Keep your head down, and keep moving forward. Decide what you want to do, learn how to do it, and take action. **Amber Jalink**

Learning From Amber's Story

All of this happened, of course, in a world where there were very few people to show you how to build an online business. Amber bought courses on sales and copywriting, and swipe files of sales letters, but she had to figure a lot out on her own. One of the biggest lessons she learned was that you can't just put something up online and hope for the best. You need to drive traffic. And that means either hiring someone to do it for you or figuring it out for yourself. Everything in business requires investment; the question is will you invest money, or will you invest your time?

Amber's biggest tip is, "Keep learning." Even if you plan to outsource a lot of what needs to be done, you should still understand the key concepts because - not surprisingly - you can end up losing money if you don't know what you're doing

Family and friends will tell you that you should get a "real" job and that it's impossible to make money online. Ignore them. Keep your head down, stay focused, and don't let yourself be distracted. Decide what you want to do, learn everything you can about it, and then take action.

The world today isn't the same as it was when Amber started her business, and it's easy to convince yourself that you've missed the boat, the world doesn't need another info publisher, or the market is saturated, and no one will buy from you. That ignores all the advantages we enjoy now compared to those early days: most homes are connected to high-speed internet; almost everyone has a PayPal account, and they're used to buying things online; and you have access to tools that didn't even exist back then and which make it possible for anyone - whatever their level of technical skill (or lack of it!) - to set up an online store and start taking payments in days rather than months.

As we've seen, life will send you challenges and test your resolve. There will be days when you think, "What am I doing? Is it worth all this hassle and heartache?" When that happens, take a day or two away from the business: read a book that has nothing to do with work, take a walk, or do whatever you need to do to disconnect. Then, when you come back, sit down - ideally away from the computer - and brainstorm. "What do I know? What can I do?" Go back through the emails you've received from customers and look for ideas - after all, that's how Amber landed on The Journal Creator!

A critical part of keeping going when things get tough is setting realistic expectations, especially when you first start. Ignore overhyped business opportunity ads that promise you can make $5,000 next week and $50,000 in the next two months. The problem with that kind of message is that it fires you up initially, but when the results don't come in as quickly as you hoped, you can just as easily get discouraged.

Yes, it can be done, but the people who can do it have usually done it before. Like Amber, they have experience and hard-earned lessons behind them. In short, they know what they're doing. So instead, set yourself a goal to make your first $100. Then go for the next $500, and $1,000 after that. Keep increasing your goals as your confidence grows.

When you need a car, don't think, "I haven't made enough." Instead, ask yourself, "How can I generate the money to buy that car?" John Lennon and Paul McCartney once famously decided to "write a swimming pool." Your attitude has to be the same. Like Amber, you can "write yourself a Lexus."

Sometimes, the tests will push you to your limits, but you have to push through whatever life throws at you. The world changes, and sometimes you will need to pivot.

For Amber, that meant moving away from selling advertising and finding new products and new markets. In 2007, the global economy collapsed. The advertisers Amber's business relied on cut their ad spend virtually overnight, and revenue plummeted from hundreds of thousands of dollars to tens of thousands.

Aaron went back to work as a network administrator, and Amber decided to look for a part-time job as a software trainer. Her husband tried to talk her out of it. He pointed out that, after a long day in the training room, she wouldn't want to sit down and start working on her business. But in the end, the Universe decided for her.

Even though Amber's resume listed everything she'd achieved in her business, and she knew Microsoft Office better than just about anybody, employers told her she wasn't qualified, and she'd been out of the workforce for "too long." The only offer Amber got was for a retail job. Luckily, it came in just as she had launched a new initiative in her business and sales were picking up. She decided she'd be losing too much if she gave up just then.

Today, Amber, Aaron, and their daughter all work in the business. Their daughter studied design at college, and now she creates all the graphics for the company. It's become a true family business.

Aside from 2007, annual revenue has consistently been over $100,000 since 2000. Today, it averages $135,000, and at the time of writing, sales had already exceeded that figure only nine months into the year.

It's not a multi-million-dollar business, but it was never intended to be. It's a lifestyle business that pays the bills and more. Last summer, the Jalinks paid for a pool in the backyard. Soon, they'll be shopping for a new car, and they'll pay cash again. And none of the family has to go out to work or worry about office politics.

As Amber's story shows, when you set your mind and your heart on something, it's totally achievable.

CHAPTER 2

Mark Walker

Mark Walker, "The Business Builder," has been in business for more than 30 years. In the late 1990s, Mark grew two of the largest eBay seller businesses (before the term Power Seller had even been created), covering gardening equipment and small electrical appliances. At one point, he had 500 product lines in a 25,000-square-foot warehouse. That's when he started studying online marketing.

While eBay was a great selling platform, and they ran TV ads that drew buyers to the site, Mark didn't like being dependent on a third party for his success. He needed to be in control of his own marketing and traffic.

Mark had bought a couple of products - the Seven-Figure Formula and Butterfly Marketing - from Mike Filsaime (founder of Butterfly Marketing, Genesis, WebinarJam, Kartra, Groove, and many other well-known companies). Initially, he applied the ideas from those courses in his own business, then he became an affiliate, promoting them to other business owners. In fact, from 2005 to 2012, Mark was one of Mike's top UK affiliates.

Over the years, Mark has become good friends with many well-known figures in the online industry - not only Mike Filsaime, but people like Daven Michaels, Joe Jablonsky, Chris Farrell, and of course, yours truly.

Today, Mark owns multiple businesses, most of which offer some form of business support, whether as a consultant helping companies expand, mentoring individuals, or providing done-for-you services. For example, one of Mark's businesses is a leaflet creation and printing service for property investors, so they don't have to learn how to use Photoshop to create, as he describes it, "great looking leaflets that generate motivated seller leads." Instead, the investor can go to his website, pick a template, and add their details. The company then prints the leaflets and ships them to the investor.

I learned a long, long time ago that it's when we support people around us that we become financially secure, financially independent, and wealthy. **Mark Walker**

In his 36 years in business, Mark has worked with hundreds of one-to-one clients and thousands more through his masterminds and the organizations he's coached. And in that time, he's helped his clients collectively generate almost £1 billion ($1.4 billion) in sales.

Mark's skill is creating businesses quickly, either from scratch or by scaling an existing business and putting multiple income streams in place (which is easy when you know what to look for). When a client hires him, he goes in not just as a "fresh pair of eyes" but as CEO, finance director, operations manager, and warehouse manager all in one, looking for opportunities to generate additional profits. He also steps into failing businesses to bring them back from the brink, which is how he ended up living in a small town in South Wales rather than London or LA.

Mark was approached by a director of a billion-dollar business that was having problems with its operations in Wales. In what sounds like an episode of Undercover Boss, he went into the company pretending to be a driver alongside the warehouse operators and the other drivers.

Unfortunately, the employees caught on very quickly: he asked too many questions and took much more interest in what was going on than a simple driver would! In the end, though, it wasn't too much of a problem, and within three months, Mark had the business back on track. The client was so impressed that they asked him to do the same at their nearby center in Bristol, England. That assignment, too, was a success, and Mark helped them secure government contracts.

After the project ended, Mark decided to stay where he was. As you'll read time and again in this book, one of the great benefits of running an info publishing business is that you can live wherever you want - you don't have to be in a major city - and your customers can be all over the world.

And to show you that an info publishing business can be resilient and succeed regardless of what's happening in the world, during COVID, Mark launched three new ventures that brought in multiple six-figures in profit. When the pandemic restrictions were lifted in the UK, those businesses were fully booked with customers through the summer and into September.

You're Never Too Young To Start A Business

Mark caught the entrepreneurial bug young: at age eight, he was charging elderly neighbors to mow their lawns and trim their hedges. Even at that early age, however, he understood the power of leverage: by the time he was nine and a half, he was paying a friend to work for him. Mark would charge his customers £5 per hour (about $7), out of which he gave his friend £3 and kept £2.

In today's digital world, it's even easier to start a business. Mark firmly believes you can be up and running online in less than an hour, and one of the keys to launching and scaling quickly without going crazy is outsourcing: hiring other people to do things you don't want to do, which they can do more cheaply than you, or which they are simply faster and more skilled at than you. That frees you up to focus on the areas where you can add the greatest value to your business.

So, if Mark is launching a new business and needs a Facebook page, he'll pay someone else to do it and give them an idea of the graphics and a script so they can create content for the next few weeks. Much like his childhood gardening business, Mark comes up with the business idea and overall strategy and pays someone else to do the equivalent of the weeding and mowing.

Dealing With Challenges

Of course, life hasn't always been smooth. At 17, Mark was running the largest nightclub in his hometown. That's where he developed his skills for growing multiple streams of income, and over the next two years, Mark took the club from opening just three nights a week to seven, with something going on every day of the week. And with success came money: at 18, he was driving a sports car he'd bought and paid for himself.

At the time, the rave music scene was taking off, and inevitably, a big, successful club got the attention of drug dealers from London and other big cities. Mark isn't into drugs - he's never even smoked a cigarette - and the club had a firm "no drugs" policy. So, he started to get threats, at first by phone, and eventually at knifepoint and gunpoint.

The final straw was when a friend warned Mark there was a hit out on him. Given that he didn't even own the club - he'd been growing it for the directors, although he'd been sharing in the profits - Mark decided enough was enough. So, he quit the club world and bought a parcel franchise.

For the next four and a half years, he and his partner (both business and life partner at the time) ran that business very successfully. Just when everything seemed to be going well, however, tragedy struck: their young son died.

Aged just 24, Mark realized it was time to reevaluate his priorities. He sold the parcel franchise for a seven-figure sum and started consulting to other franchise owners. It was a very fast-moving and evolving industry. When the French government bought a bankrupt parcel carrier in Britain, Mark was hired to turn that business around. He was also instrumental in many other acquisitions and mergers of parcel companies across the United Kingdom and closing down businesses if he saw they weren't going anywhere and the owners should cut their losses.

And all of that was while Mark was still in his 20s.

After 36 years in business, Mark has a lot of experience to share, and even though he's in the information industry, he doesn't always charge for it.

Why? First, because much of that information and experience came to him for free, and if he can filter that information, he can give someone a better, faster start in their own business.

Second, he knows that the key to success in business is to create value for others, and one way to do that is to share your experience freely. That's a message you'll see repeatedly in this book, and it's also central to how Kate and I run our business.

The free information Nick and Kate give away in their emails and their membership is absolutely incredible. So for anybody reading this, you need to follow Nick and Kate James. **Mark Walker**

Mark is a subscriber to my internet marketing newsletter monthly PLR. In many ways. It's another example of him outsourcing tasks to people who do something well. Creating content is one of the biggest blocks and time-sucks for many new marketers, and the PLR newsletter is a simple way to break through that block and get that time back. The idea of the newsletter is that our clients can take it and rebrand it as their own.

It takes a lot of time and effort to create content and interview guest experts for a newsletter like the one Nick and Kate James run. So when I came across it, I snapped it up. It's top-notch information for anybody who wants to understand how to get into internet marketing and make a living from it. Whether you're new to the industry or more experienced and looking for a refresher, you should subscribe as quickly as you can. **Mark Walker**

Plans For The Future

Mark is always looking for new opportunities. When we interviewed him for this book, he had just launched a business that helps homeowners get a refund on their mortgage payments if the mortgage has been securitized and sold to a third party without their knowledge. He's already registered 40,000 claims. Again, it's a service that helps customers do something they can't do themselves: he's not making widgets and hoping he can sell them for more than they cost to produce.

A second business is Property Lotto, which Mark sees as his "legacy" company. It's a partnership with a well-known lawyer and another partner to set up a draw with a £200,000 ($270,000) prize which the winner can use to either buy a new home or pay off their existing mortgage.

Mark compares starting a new business to buying wine in the supermarket. Do you buy a bottle for $50 and drink it, or set up a company that makes $50 and use that money to pay for the wine - effectively making it free? Of course, you should set up the business. Once you drink the wine, it's gone. But the business will keep making $50 over and over and supply you with more wine for a long time to come!

Protecting Yourself In Partnerships

Mark also has JVs with past clients who have asked him to partner with them and continue as their sounding board and mentor. Over the years, Mark has had many business partners, and while most of those relationships have gone well, others have not.

By nature, Mark is a trusting person - his instinct when he meets a potential collaborator is to trust them and bring them into his business. However, he's also aware that not every alliance will work out. So, you need to be mindful of the possibility that things won't turn out as you expect and find ways to protect yourself, mitigate the risk, and lessen the impact.

Just as important as protecting yourself financially, however, is protecting your reputation. The important thing in any relationship is how it ends, and it's vital in business to leave partnerships as amicably as possible. After all, these days, you leave digital footprints for everything you do. People will Google your name, and they'll make a snap judgment - right or wrong - based on what they find, often without ever having met you.

There's a mantra in business, "hire fast, fire faster," and although it was written about taking on new staff, it applies to any business relationship. As an entrepreneur, you can't afford to carry deadwood. So, if you realize early on that someone has muscled their way into your business life and they're not doing what they said they would, you need to get them out as quickly and amicably as possible.

The Positive Power Of "No"

One of the most powerful words in business, according to Mark, is "no." We tend to see it as a negative word, but it can be very positive and freeing, especially in business. Often, people who won't say "no" are simply trying to ingratiate themselves or feeding their need to be liked at all costs (or they say "Yes," but they don't follow through because they didn't really agree with what was being said). So, if Mark gives a client or a team an idea, he'd rather they say, "No, Mark. That's not going to work." That opens up the conversation and often leads to ideas that otherwise wouldn't have come out.

Finding Balance

When you start a business, you'll initially be swapping your nine-to-five job for working on your business or thinking about it 24/7. If that's not OK for you, don't become an entrepreneur.

An entrepreneur is never truly off duty: you're always watching what's happening in the business, and you're always on the hook for something. In Mark's case, he might have to respond to a comment from someone on something he posted six years ago, or he might get an email complaining that a URL isn't working in a book he gave out as a lead magnet ten years ago.

Fortunately, it's only a passing phase and things will get easier. If that were not the case, Mark couldn't run as many businesses as he does. When you successfully outsource everything you can and condense the rest, you don't have to be in the business nine-to-five every day of the week. That's how you can create a lifestyle many people never achieve, where you can spend time doing what you love outside your business.

As well as his consulting and coaching business, Mark and his family own a property investment business that is one of the largest private landlords in his region. As with his other companies, Mark is the COO and outsources much of the day-to-day work to staff and contractors. On the back of it, Mark also runs another business that teaches people to become property investors.

However, even with that, his other JVs and companies, and his training, mentoring, and consulting activities, Mark only works three days a week. The rest of the time is his own.

The Importance Of Good Health

A theme you'll see throughout this book is the importance of health and lifestyle. Unfortunately, it's something many entrepreneurs ignore. Instead, they keep telling themselves, "There'll be time to rest when I've made my millions."

Tragedy affects people in many ways, but in Mark's case, he has taken it and used it to empower him. He embraces the now, enjoys his time, and uses his experiences to help others.

Mark has lost six friends to cancer in the last few years, so staying in good health is essential to him. He's not a gym bunny - he enjoys the finer things in life like good food, fine wines, etc. - but he balances that with looking after himself.

And mental health is as important as physical health (as you'll see in several other chapters). Mark is no stranger to tragedy. As well as losing his son early in life, he lost the child's mother to a brain tumor in 2012. That was a huge loss for him: she was older than him and had been his first mentor; even after they sold the parcel franchise and split up as a couple, they had stayed friends.

Then, in 2016, Mark's daughter from another relationship also developed a brain tumor. At the time, there was a brand-new treatment that was only available in North America. Fortunately, Mark was able to pay for the experimental treatment and fly his daughter across the Atlantic to get it. His daughter survived, but Mark took six months off from his businesses to support her through her treatment and recovery.

Two things made all that possible. First, the financial success and security that Mark had built up through his business allowed him to pay for the best treatment available and fly his daughter wherever he needed to. It also meant he could step away from his companies knowing that the bills would be taken care of, and his lifestyle wouldn't be affected. Second, the fact that Mark delegates and outsources as much as he can to experts made it possible to take that time off knowing that he'd still have a business to come back to when it was all over.

Starting a business is the biggest personal development project you'll undertake. Even if you don't have the strength you need within you, you can find it from someone else, and they will give you what you need to pull yourself through whatever is going on. **Mark Walker**

Learning From Mentors

We all come into the world the same - no one pops out of the womb with a handful of Bitcoin. Even though Mark was born into a family that has run businesses for hundreds of years, he doesn't see that as a golden ticket. Instead, he believes it just gave him more experience and knowledge to share with others and help them to accelerate their own business journey. That was why he chose to become a business mentor.

Mark also works with a business mentor himself, and he is a great believer in the power of being in a mastermind group where people can share ideas openly and freely without the fear that someone will jump in and tell them their plain is crazy or it'll never work. However experienced or successful you become, if you're a business owner, you should get a coach or join a mastermind group. Or, better yet, both! Because there is always something to be learned, and there is always value in having someone more experienced you can turn to when you hit a block.

If you want success in a shorter space of time, you can have all my books off my shelf and spend the next 36 years trying to learn from my mistakes, or you can reach out to people like Nick and Kate James. **Mark Walker**

If You're Still On The Fence

If you're reading this and still wondering whether you should take the leap of faith to start your own business, Mark's advice is simple. Remember that, as a business owner, you have a responsibility to your family - their future is riding on your business idea, too. So, before you quit your day job and start living off savings, make sure you sense-check your business idea first with someone you trust. That's not family or friends (unless they happen to be incredibly successful info publishers in their own right!): if someone is still stuck in the nine-to-five world, trading time for money, it's hard for them to understand what you're trying to do.

Mark also advises you to beware of anyone who simply left a nine-to-five job and bought a franchise as a business coach or consultant. Often, the only business these people have owned is that franchise, so they are not talking from experience.

Instead, as many of the other experts in this book recommend, find a business mentor who has already trodden the path you want to follow. The most successful mentors and coaches will often give you some of their time as a way of paying things forward, and you can reach them through LinkedIn and other social media. Those people - the ones who will make time to chat to you - are the ones you can trust from day one. They may even end up investing in your business idea!

CHAPTER 3

Alex Welsh

Alex Welsh is an excellent example of the freedom info publishing gives you to live and work wherever you want. Originally from the UK, Alex decided to move somewhere sunnier and now lives in Malaga in Southern Spain.

Like many people - including everyone reading this book (*yes, I'm looking at you!*) - Alex wanted to start an online business. As far back as 2005, he kept seeing people who seemed to be doing very well with web-based businesses, and he became a self-confessed "opportunity junkie" looking for ways to make money. After a while, he started dabbling in the online world and tried several of the most popular approaches to making money - dropshipping from China, FBA, affiliate marketing - unfortunately without much success.

However, the more books he read and videos he watched, the more Alex kept coming across the idea that the key to making money is to share your knowledge and create real value for people. And when he asked himself, "What skills do I have that I can share with people?" he came up with two potential answers.

Alex is a close-up magician, so one possibility was to teach magic tricks online. However, he didn't want hassle from other magicians for revealing the secrets of the craft, so he decided that wasn't a good area to pursue.

(On a side note, it's up to you whether you think that's a good reason for not following that path. Many people have built solid businesses by giving away "trade secrets" even when it makes their competitors angry. In fact, I'd argue that applies in every industry, even magic: a Google search for "close-up magic course online" gives 435,000 results, including masterclasses by TV magicians Penn and Teller, courses on Udemy and Skillshare, and Magic Stream ("the Netflix of Magic"), a $10-a-month subscription program with thousands of subscribers who pay for access to a massive (and expanding) library of detailed instructional videos from successful magicians.)

If it wasn't going to be magic, that left Alex's other big area of expertise: he had built a business as a locksmith, and he realized there was money to be made teaching people how to set up a locksmith business. So, he created Locksmithing Secrets, an online course that teaches both the technical skills (e.g., fitting, changing, and even picking a lock; how to open cars and program car keys, etc.) and the business skills they need.

As well as access to the lessons, however, buyers also get an online community on Facebook and WhatsApp. The community means students can learn from each other all the time, which takes the pressure off Alex to constantly create new material (something you should consider for your own info publishing business!).

Getting Started

Alex started by creating free instructional videos on YouTube. That allowed him to see how much of an opportunity there was and do some free market research about how many people watched, whether they engaged, whether they subscribed to his channel, which topics got the most traction, etc.

One thing you often hear in marketing is not to create something totally new; that it's safer to stick to niches where there's already some competition because it proves that there's money to be made in that business. When Alex started researching his business idea, he discovered there were no other online courses for locksmiths. He wondered if he was crazy trying to create a whole new industry online, but he decided to go ahead and try anyway.

Today, Alex makes more from his info publishing business than he did as a locksmith. Each month, the site averages $5,000 in sales - all on autopilot - and he does very little apart from sending an email now and then, leaving plenty of time for other interests (including, of course, magic!).

Of course, it wasn't that successful right from day one; Alex didn't just launch a site and immediately start making hundreds of sales. He has grown the business over time by implementing fundamental strategies that he learned from my books and courses, like split testing and optimization, and tweaking his site and offers.

Nick is big on three things: driving traffic, optimizing your sales funnel, and getting the most value out of each customer. And when Nick speaks, I listen. **Alex Welsh**

Working Wherever You Want

Part of the motivation for setting up an info publishing business was Alex's long-standing dream of moving to Spain. He'd visited the country many times to do magic gigs, and initially, he wanted to move out there to be a full-time close-up magician. However, the language barrier and the lack of consistent work for entertainers forced him to set that idea aside. Fortunately, neither of those is a problem in the info publishing industry! Once Alex got himself out of the mindset we're all pushed into at school - trading time for money working for someone else - and wrapped his head around the idea of creating a product once and selling it over and over again, he put all his energy into building an online business.

And as Alex puts it, "once you make your first sale online, it's hard to look back."

Alex launched the business in 2020, just before he emigrated, and at first, he made one or two sales each week. Not long after, the Pandemic started and Spain went into lockdown. Many people would see that as a disaster. Instead, Alex saw it as an opportunity to focus entirely on getting his online business up and running: he could work ten hours a day without distractions and teach himself everything he needed to know about marketing and the web.

Of course, Alex had a strong motivation: if he couldn't make the business work, he wouldn't be able to survive in Spain, and he'd soon be on a flight back to Britain!

Finding Support And Guidance

Like many new entrepreneurs, Alex did a lot of reading (including my book Six-Figures a Year in Info Publishing). He also bought several of my training programs and hired me as his business coach.

One of the big lessons Alex took from my programs - apart from the need to split test everything and keep tweaking and optimizing, which we've already mentioned - is the importance of simplicity and clarity in copywriting. A confused shopper doesn't buy. So, you need to make your copy clear and understandable.

I've always studied Nick's work, and I really admire his copywriting. It's very simple and straight to the point. **Alex Welsh**

The rush you get from your first sale is addictive. Alex uses Stripe to process payments, and every time he makes a sale, he gets a notification. One night, he was out having dinner with friends, and the phone kept pinging every few minutes. His friends asked what was going on, and when he told them it was sales happening while he was out eating, they all wanted to know how to set up an info publishing business for themselves.

Once you've had an experience like that, it's hard to even think about going back to a 9-to-5 job.

Before Alex started his online business, he had fallen out of love with locksmithing. Many of the jobs that came his way were to accompany court officials and help them enter properties to enforce a court order. As you can imagine, those were very confrontational, high-stress situations.

And as a locksmith, Alex couldn't just turn off his phone at the end of a 10-hour workday. He was on-call 24/7 to homeowners and business owners for emergencies. And Alex doesn't like letting anyone down, so if the phone rang at 3 a.m., he'd grab his tools and get in his car.

The irony, of course, is that today Alex makes much more money while working a lot less. One of the first things he thinks of when he wakes up each morning is how great it is that he made money in his sleep, like a rock star living off royalties. Sometimes, he looks at how many sales came in overnight and has to pinch himself to prove it isn't all a dream.

> *Part of the secret to being happy in business is gratitude. Every day, I'm grateful that I got to make sales and I didn't have to work for them. It's a great feeling!* **Alex Welsh**

When he first created his course, Alex focused only on the domestic locksmith market, teaching how to work with door locks for houses and businesses. But he kept hearing - from me and others - that he needed an upsell. When someone is going through your funnel, there should always be ways for them to spend more money. Of course, not everyone will take everything you put in front of them, but if the offer isn't there, the only thing you can guarantee is that you won't make money!

The first add-on product Alex created was a course on how to work on car locks, and he was blown away by the conversion rate: 70% of people who bought the basic offer added the upsell! Then people started emailing to ask whether they could just buy the upsell.

Alex realized that the auto course was actually the key selling point of what he was teaching. So, he switched the offers to make that the first thing people could buy and turned the domestic course into an upsell. It turned out to be a genius move because sales skyrocketed.

Where To Focus

Like most new entrepreneurs, he focused on sales when Alex started his business. However, as the business grew and became more established, he shifted his focus to stability. It's one thing to have a great month every so often, but the key to business success is ensuring every month is great. Business is full of uncertainty: you could wake up one day and find YouTube has shut down your channel or Facebook has banned your ads. Google could change their algorithm, and instead of showing up on page one, suddenly you're on page 157 (it's happened!), or the cost of pay-per-click ads could go through the roof suddenly. The best way to insulate yourself from what the outside world is doing is to create sources of predictable repeat income in your business.

During a consulting session with Alex, he asked me how to expand the funnel even more. The big thing missing from his business model was recurring income. But I pointed out that he didn't need to create anything new for this: he already had the perfect membership offer in his business. The next day, Alex started charging a monthly subscription for access to the online community he'd been giving away as part of the program.

> *Since working with Nick, I've really optimized my online business. Not only that, but I've been able to add continuity income, which has given me not only a huge hike in sales but also a lot of peace of mind and stability. Nick took the time to look at my online business, and everything he's shown me has really helped: even minor tweaks have had a huge positive effect on my business.* **Alex Welsh**

Alex was also getting requests from new locksmiths for help setting up their website, which presented another opportunity for continuity income. So he introduced a service where he builds their site for free and charges them a monthly fee for hosting, maintenance, and running costs.

These sources of recurring revenue give Alex great peace of mind. Even when you're making sales daily, you never know how much you'll sell from week to week. There are good days and bad days, good months and bad months. However, with the membership and website fees, Alex knows in advance precisely how much money will come in each month.

It's as close to guaranteed income as you can get in business: once you know how many people join each month and how long they stay in your program on average, you can predict your revenue months in advance And, if something unexpected happens, you have time to make corrections and adjust.

Dealing With Doubters

Some people really struggle to understand the idea of an info publishing business - especially the older generation who were brought up believing you get a job, work 9-to-5, and put money in a pension plan. Even now, many people still don't believe you can make money online, and they don't see info publishing as a "real" or legitimate career path. So, when you share your plans, the chances are you'll meet some uninformed resistance.

When he started the business, Alex was lucky that most people around him were supportive. But, of course, there were still a few naysayers. For example, someone would see him reading a book about making money online and say, "It's all a scam. Stop wasting your time and money. You're not going to get rich from that."

Alex got through it by staying focused and not paying attention to the negativity. He's always been a determined person, and when he sets a goal, he goes for it. His advice, if you're considering starting an info publishing business, is to believe in what you're doing and not to listen to other people's opinions, even close friends and family. It's not that they have bad intentions. Usually, the advice comes from a desire to protect you from what they see - based on their limited experience - as a risk. But, of course, the best antidote is when you make the first few sales, and you see for yourself that you're building a real business.

> *If you're going to listen to someone, listen to someone who's already done what you want to do. Find mentors and role models you can look up to, and take advice from them, not from people who haven't done what you want to do.* **Alex Welsh**

Life As An Info Publisher

Alex admits he did suffer from stress back when he was a locksmith in the UK. Like many owners of "normal" businesses, Alex believed he was his own boss. In reality, however, he had hundreds of bosses: his customers. When you're a locksmith, everything is an emergency. Whether someone has lost their key or their lock has broken, they want the problem solved immediately. So, Alex was constantly rushing from job to job.

Two days before his 30th birthday, Alex lost his father. Instead of taking time to grieve, he threw himself even more into his locksmith business and bottled up all the emotions. But, of course, as you'll see in many chapters in this book, those negative emotions can't be kept back forever; eventually, they find a way out.

Like Michael Wilding, Alex began having panic attacks while he was working. Alex needed to take a step back and live life at a slower pace. So, having the freedom to move somewhere calmer - the freedom that comes with running an info publishing business - was a gift.

As an info publisher, life is much less stressful. In fact, Alex describes it as zero stress! Of course, it helps that he lives in a country known for sunshine and a very laid-back way of life, but really, it's about the business.

On a typical day, Alex wakes up, checks how many sales came in overnight, replies to any questions that have come in by email, and sends a quick marketing email to his list. After that, he heads to the gym or the sauna until lunchtime. After lunch, he'll work on the business, checking stats, optimizing the site or the funnel, or working on marketing, and in the evening, he'll go out for drinks or a meal with friends.

Alex also has plenty of time for trips away exploring Spain and Europe (lockdowns and pandemics permitting!), and thanks to his business, he has bought his first house in Spain, paid for by his income from info publishing.

Maybe the next stage of the business will be for Alex to "write himself a swimming pool" (just as Amber Jalink "wrote herself a Lexus" by creating and launching her new product).

The Temptation To Go Back

At some point in their journey, many business owners may be tempted to go back to their old life. That's not the case for Alex.

For him, there's no return. Even if something happened and Locksmithing Secrets collapsed overnight, Alex knows he has the skills to allow him to start another online business. And thanks to the success he's enjoyed in just two years, he has the confidence to do it, too.

Advice If You're Considering Starting An Info Publishing Business

If you're still on the fence about setting up an info publishing business, Alex's advice is to just get started. The great thing about this industry is that you don't have to quit your job and go all-in. Instead, you can keep working at whatever you do, so you still have income, but focus every other waking hour on your business.

One handy tip from Alex is not to go into this thinking, "I want to make $100,000 a year." Instead, put all your effort into making just the first sale - the one that proves that other people want what you're selling. Once you've got that proof of concept, you can keep repeating it and grow your business to whatever you want it to be.

CHAPTER 4

Matt Garrett

Matt Garrett used to sell software to attorneys. It was a job that kept him constantly on the road with a lifestyle he hated. As an info publisher, however, he gets to work from home and loves it. When the COVID lockdowns started in 2020, many people struggled with remote working, especially staying focused with family around them. For Matt and others like him, it was just business as usual - and of course, many people get into info publishing specifically to be around their family.

Like many marketers, Matt has many irons in the fire. A large part of his business is creating new products and launching them: over the last ten years, he has launched or relaunched over a hundred products, alone or with JV partners. He's also an active blogger, and he coaches other entrepreneurs on how to create and launch their own products.

Another of his business activities is managing email lists for other info publishers: a well-managed mailing list is the most valuable asset you can have in your business, giving you consistent, recurring income that you control. However, many entrepreneurs don't run their list well - they ignore the basics like maintaining regular communication and performing routine maintenance such as removing unresponsive leads. Over time, problems arise that can reduce your deliverability (the proportion of your emails that make it into people's inboxes rather than ending up in Spam) or even get you blocked altogether.

Many marketers are afraid of emailing their list in case they come across as pushy or salesy, or they just don't know what to write. But, after doing email marketing for 15 years, Matt has sent thousands of emails. So, he knows a thing or two about it, and over the last few years, more and more marketers have asked him to manage their email marketing for them.

In total, Matt's businesses generate a steady $400,000 per year, and although part of that revenue is shared with his JV partners, he still makes multiple six-figures each year. His flagship product is a recurring monthly membership that teaches people how to start and grow an online business by creating a blog, getting into a content-writing routine, building a list, and launching their own product. Another of his products has made over $500,000 since its launch in 2011. His other main business is a JV with another info publisher: the company provides high-quality WordPress plugins and accompanying tutorials, and Matt aims to build that brand in the coming years.

Getting Into Info Publishing

As I mentioned above, Matt's career before info publishing was selling software to law offices. He was always on the road, and it wasn't unusual for him to rack up 50,000 miles in a year driving between cities to demonstrate the software. One significant benefit of his job, however, was that he could work from home rather than an office. In his spare time, he started dabbling on the internet, and soon his friends began asking him for advice on things like online security.

These days, firewall software is built into your computer's operating system, but back in 2000, you needed separate tools. One of those security systems was called Zone Alarm Pro, and it was the one that Matt always recommended to his friends. Rather than keep emailing people the link to the company's sales page, Matt added it to his homepage so he could send friends to his website and tell them to click the link.

One day, he was on Zone Alarm Pro's site, and he spotted a link at the bottom of their page labeled Partners. That was his introduction to the world of affiliate marketing, and it allowed him to monetize the advice he was already giving. After a while, Matt realized he could probably get more targeted traffic if he set up a website specifically about the product. So, he contacted the company and asked their permission to register the domain *zone-alarm.co.uk*. They agreed, and he bought that domain and a few similar ones.

Matt started by building simple one- or two-page review sites on different servers and linking them together (a popular SEO technique at the time). Eventually, he discovered the affiliate platform ClickBank and found other products with even better affiliate programs. Before he knew it, Matt was earning more from his side hustle than from his day job. In fact, by 2005, his online income was more than double his salary (which was already high to start with), and he decided it was time to quit his job.

Matt's job had always been home-based, but it wasn't until he worked 100% from home that he realized just how much time he had lost in the car. Initially, when he got the sales job, Matt thought it was great: he'd spend seven hours listening to music or audiobooks as he drove, do an hour or two of 'real' work demoing the software, and get paid for the whole day. But when he started to work for himself, he realized the drive was dead time when he could instead have been creating valuable content, writing new products, building his list, or whatever.

The big thing missing in Matt's life as an employee, however, was control. Many entrepreneurs get into business because they have a burning desire to be able to do what they want, be in control, and live life on their own terms. For Matt, that turns up even in the little details. For example, in the last ten years, he has only worn a suit at weddings. On Monday mornings, he hardly ever gets up before noon - he prefers to work later in the day when he is happier and more productive.

Whatever you want or don't want in your life, being an info publisher is genuinely liberating because you get to decide on your own work-life balance, and you don't have to take orders from anyone else. That can make it hard to go back to being an employee - Matt freely admits he'd struggle to work for a boss these days because they'd end up arguing. He's too used to doing things his own way.

It's Not All "Sunshine And Unicorns"

Matt has been through two divorces. His first marriage lasted seven years, but one day his wife told him she didn't believe he'd ever be successful in building a business or be a millionaire. That lack of vision and faith destroyed the relationship.

Matt's second wife also had trouble adjusting to being married to an entrepreneur (though she eventually bought into the idea). One of the affiliate businesses Matt had been running was for a Russian mail-order bride company, and he ended up marrying one of their brides. The problem was that she came from a background where the man's role was to go out to work 9-to-5, Monday to Friday, and bring home money. At first, she just couldn't get used to the idea that Matt was sitting at home all day on the computer and working odd hours.

She did adapt, but unfortunately, the good times didn't last. The business was going very well - monthly AdSense commission payments were over $10,000 - and Matt decided the best way to scale rapidly would be to bring on three other marketers as partners. However, some of the techniques they used fell afoul of Google's terms of service, and their accounts got blocked.

Overnight, the business went from very successful to flatlining. Worse, there was no notification of what had happened, and Google paid commissions 60 days in arrears. So, for two months, Matt and his partners continued pouring money into driving traffic, unaware that their accounts had been blacklisted and they wouldn't be getting any commission. It was a painful lesson, but Matt has steered clear of "black hat" strategies ever since.

All of this coincided with marital problems, and Matt ended up having to rebuild his business while simultaneously dealing with financial difficulties and going through his second divorce. It was a dark time. For two and a half years, Matt's life revolved around playing World of Warcraft, doing some blogging, emailing his list, and getting drunk. His kids became the bedrock of his life - he would see them every other weekend, which was the only thing that kept him sane and got him through that time.

When Life Gives You Lemons

As odd as it may seem, there was an upside to all this. After 20 months of playing, Matt got to know World of Warcraft really well; so well, in fact, that he wrote a book about the game and launched it on ClickBank - it was the first time he offered a product of his own for other people to promote.

Back then, books were a popular offer on ClickBank, and it made him a lot of money. More importantly, it taught him the value of building a list. Matt's business model until then had been simple - drive traffic to a website and put affiliate offers in front of them - but there was no back end. Once someone clicked a link or left the site, there was no way to follow up and put other offers in front of them.

But now, the list Matt had built selling copies of the book kept the business going: it kept the lights on, put food on the table, and paid his subscriptions to World of Warcraft.

Then, in 2007, Matt launched another ebook, Lazy Git Marketing, and made $30,000 in sales in a week. And he made 3x as much income again in the following months by marketing to the list of buyers he built in that week. That was what convinced him to put his energy into list building and email marketing.

In your business life, you will make mistakes. There will be pain, but you will learn from that pain. When Matt emerged from his "dark period" (as he calls it), he teamed up again with one of his earlier business partners. They had been chatting about blogging and keyword research for SEO, and Matt realized his ex-partner could probably build software to automate a lot of what Matt was doing by hand in his blog posts. That software was launched in 2011, and in one week, the pair signed up 1,100 subscribers at $67 per month.

In a very short time, Matt went from hardship and misery to success. He finally remembered what the ups were like, and it turned him around: he started to enjoy building products and growing the business again.

The Power Of Community

For Matt, one of the biggest positives of the last few years has been the friendships he has made in the info publishing world. Entrepreneurship can be lonely: you sit at your computer on your own rather than in an office with other people. On top of that, there's the pressure of knowing that your happiness and the security of your family hinge entirely on your ability to launch a new product, build a list, pick the right JV or affiliate offer, etc.

That pressure can get to you and grind you down. You need to find healthy ways to deal with it - booze and World of Warcraft don't count - and one of the best ways is to talk things through with other people.

When things aren't going well, it's critical to have a support network of fellow marketers you can reach out to for advice or to discuss what's going on without fear of judgment. You need to surround yourself with friends who understand what you're doing, because there will be many other people in your life who don't get it. For some, what you're doing is so far outside their experience and their model of the world that they will be afraid you're making a terrible mistake - and that fear can be contagious. Others may be terrified that you will succeed, and you'll move on and leave them behind.

When Matt quit his sales job, many of his friends thought he was crazy for leaving a very well-paid job to work online - and most of them didn't believe it would work (of course, these days, they get it!). But he made new friends in the online business world - people he met at events or connected with because they are in similar niches - which has given him a peer group who understand the business. He can talk to them about EPC, ROI, conversion rates, and split testing without their eyes glazing over, and many of them have even turned into JV partners or affiliates.

Along his journey, Matt has met many friends who don't just help and support him but inspire him, like Simon Hodgkinson and Simon Jordanson. He also follows successful marketers like Igor Kheifets, Eric Louviere, and John Thornhill. Matt has even started organizing get-togethers for successful marketers. It's a great excuse to get his industry friends together regularly for dinner or drinks - and you never know when someone will say something around the table that sparks an idea for a new business or suggests the answer to a complex business challenge.

Keeping Healthy, Focused, And Motivated

Most "how to get started in business online" books don't talk about how to stay healthy. Working long hours at your computer day after day - especially in the early stages - can take its toll if you don't build healthy habits into your life.

Matt has created a regular daily routine that he finds suits him and helps him make the most of every day, and my advice to you would be to figure out what works for you - and always remember to consult a medical professional before making any major lifestyle or diet changes.

Matt's morning starts with a hot shower, and he turns it down to cold for the last minute or so to wake himself up. That's followed by some exercise, then a meditation to work on his self-talk and mindset.

Matt continues his day with hot lemon water and apple cider vinegar, and he has replaced caffeinated drinks with green tea or plain water. During the week, he practices intermittent fasting, and on weekends he allows himself a little wine in the evening.

He also knows that he has an addictive personality, and he can get hooked on things very quickly. When he worked in sales, he survived on coffee and cigarettes, and as we saw above, during his 'dark days,' he threw himself into World of Warcraft and alcohol. If he did go out, it would be to go to the shops or meet friends at the pub to get drunk. Either way, he didn't get much daylight! So, these days, along with giving up coffee and cigarettes, Matt makes sure to schedule time every day to get fresh air and sunlight - and that, combined with exercise in the morning, has been the most significant factor in maintaining his physical and psychological health.

And because he does enjoy gaming, Matt has built an outlet for that into his life by allowing two or three hours a day to play Pokémon GO, which he treats as an exercise app! He knows he'll walk at least 30 miles (50 km) each week chasing Pokémons. During that time, he also listens to audiobooks, so his brain gets a workout as well as his body. He even met his fiancée through the game, so there are other benefits! In effect, Matt has found a way to make exercise and personal development fun in a way that taps into his personality, which is critical when your life revolves around a screen and a keyboard.

One of the few benefits of an addictive personality is that the addiction can also apply to activities, making it much easier for

Matt to get into a state of focus and flow and stay there. He also uses music to enhance that focus - perhaps not surprisingly, Matt listens to game soundtracks when he's working, but it's not because of his love of gaming. Game music is engineered to draw your attention into a game and keep you focused. So, even if he's not playing, Matt finds it helps him get his work done.

The secret is to find specific pieces or a genre that will put you in the right state of mind. Create a playlist, and when it's time to work, turn that on, switch off all the notifications from apps and devices, close your eyes for a moment to focus, and when you're ready, open your eyes and get to work.

Staying Focused

There's a lot to do in info publishing, and success requires a level of focus, dedication, and motivation that most people simply don't have. Apart from using music to keep himself in flow, Matt has work routines and systems he follows. For example, at the end of each day, he lists his top priorities for the following day. That way, when he sits down the next morning, he knows what to work on rather than sitting there trying to think of something to do.

One of the most powerful ways Matt has found to start the day well and get down to business quickly is to pick one item on his to-do list and get it done. For this, Matt uses the Pomodoro technique: he sets a timer for 25 minutes and focuses exclusively on that single task. When the timer goes off, he takes a five-minute break and then sets another 25-minute timer.

Working like that, Matt can easily get through half of his to-do list (or more) in a few hours. Then, throughout the day, as Matt completes more items on the list, he crosses them out.

Often, in business, you'll reach the end of a week wondering whether you got anything done, not even knowing whether it was a good or bad week. When that happens, Matt can look back through his lists and see whether he can congratulate himself on a productive week or if he missed his targets, in which case he can hold himself accountable.

Matt also makes a list at the start of each month of his priorities for that month, and he reviews those each quarter to ensure the business is progressing.

Matt makes lists at different levels. He has one book with big-picture tasks, for example setting up YouTube paid ads for a new product. Then, in a separate notebook, he'll break down each of those major to-dos into the individual steps needed to make that happen and assign due dates to each one.

A valuable lesson Matt has learned is to be flexible - it can be hard to hit exact dates, especially when you're working on multiple tasks simultaneously. So, the lists are really there to keep him focused. And over the years, Matt has kept all his 'little black books' of lists, so he has a complete record of everything he has done to grow the business and everything he has achieved.

The Biggest Challenge

For any entrepreneur, one of the biggest challenges is lack of time. Ultimately, you just have to accept that you'll never get everything done in the time available. So, one of the most critical skills for you to develop is prioritization (and the ability to reprioritize on the fly!). And two things you absolutely must make time for - whatever else is happening in your life or business - are health and personal relationships.

After that, you'll be juggling product creation, list building, marketing, building partnerships, driving traffic, and all the rest. Getting an automated funnel set up with paid traffic can take some of the pressure off as you are less dependent on launches and finding new JVs and traffic sources. One of Matt's friends, Eric Louviere, likens it to a juggling octopus on roller skates.

A critical way of creating more time is outsourcing tasks to VAs and contractors, which Matt is actively working on. However, you can't just hire someone and say, "Make this happen!" For example, Matt wants to get a VA to handle paid traffic for his business. So first, he has to record videos that lay out the processes step-by-step in a way that's easy to understand. Of course, that means he has to understand the topic thoroughly himself, which means taking time to study it in-depth.

Luckily, teaching a VA is the same as teaching a client, so those videos eventually become products he can sell - another secret for finding more time as an info publisher: look for ways to repurpose and monetize everything you create and do.

If You're Considering A Career In Info Publishing

Matt's advice for anyone thinking of getting started in info publishing goes back to what we've already said in this chapter.

First, get out and meet people. Attending events is a great way to do this because you never know who will be there or who you'll end up working with. And don't be afraid to partner with other people. It's hard to do everything and be an expert at all the skills you need in business, and partnerships are a great way to round out your experience and fill the gaps in your knowledge, especially when you hit a roadblock. For example, Matt's partner in the WordPress business is a coder: he has a coder's mindset, and he's great at fixing software problems. That's not Matt's wheelhouse. Their skills are different and complementary, so they can talk to each other when they're stuck and help each other out. That's why they work well together.

Matt has had seven or eight different business partners over the years. It didn't always work out, but that's life. Overall, his experiences collaborating with others have been fantastic, and they have made him a lot of money.

Some of the people you meet may become accountability partners instead. For example, if you connect with two or three people at an event, arrange to meet online weekly or monthly to talk through your goals and hold each other accountable. That can make a massive difference to your ability to implement because you're no longer just thinking, "I want to do X"; you're telling someone else, so you're more likely to get it done. And if you get stuck, they'll probably be able to help you.

Second, build an email list. Any time someone encounters you online, there should be a way for you to add their contact details to your mailing list because that will be your best source of income. In fact, your email list is your business - remember that thanks to his list, Matt was able to keep himself going for three years. There are many ways to build a business, but most of them boil down to building an audience to which you can promote offers, whether your own or someone else's. An email list is far more responsive than a Facebook group or anything like that, and you have total control over it: with other people's platforms, you're always subject to their rules and whims. One day, a moderator on one of your social media platforms could decide they don't like what you're doing and shut down your account - usually with little or no recourse or right to appeal - and if that's all you have, then your business is back to zero.

Third, make sure you look after your physical and mental health. Schedule time for exercise, fresh air and daylight, and eat well. You don't have to be a monk or a health freak - Matt still enjoys a few glasses of wine - but keep things under control.

Fourth, try as many ways as you can think of to make money in your business. Don't focus on a particular business model until you know which ones you like, and which work best for you. The flip side of that is that, at some point, you will need to focus on one core thing that you put more time and effort into than others and which will generate a solid return.

Fifth, and finally, find a good coach and mentor. Even though it can be expensive, it can save you thousands in the long run because it's easy to go in the wrong direction if you're on your own, pour money into the wrong things, and end up spinning your wheels and not getting anywhere. Finding someone who has a system that works will always be the quickest route to success because if they're willing to show you exactly what works and help you get it up and running, it makes things far quicker and easier. Most people starting in info publishing do it as a sideline, so they still have a full-time job, and their time is even more precious and limited. Others do it because they've been laid off or lost their job, and they need to get up and running quickly. If you're in either of those situations, you need to be on a proven path and follow a mentor who can say, *"This is what you need to do!"* and lay out the exact steps.

CHAPTER 5

David Greis

Davis Greis from Long Island, NY, has always loved to write. So, it was inevitable that he'd find his way into info publishing as a career. And David is a prolific content creator: as I write, he has three live products and two more upcoming launches.

David started his publishing journey 30 years ago. As a Customer Manager for a window company, he was sent on many courses on customer service and relationship management. Most people see corporate training as a chore; just one more box to check for HR. David chose instead to be inspired. This was back when corporate training still happened in classrooms, not online, and he realized that if his company thought those courses were worth paying for and taking him away from work for several days, there must be value in them - and a market.

David has always been an entrepreneur. Even as a child, he created side hustles to bring in money. In high school, he mowed lawns like a lot of kids. He also started a business, Western Hemisphere Electronics, fixing televisions and stereos with a friend (and when he set up his current company, he called it Western Hemisphere Enterprises and used the same logo in memory of that childhood initiative).

Now, David is the kind of person who is willing to learn and try new things. For example, when he and his wife wanted an addition to the house, he taught himself the skills he needed - carpentry, brickwork, plumbing, electrical work, etc. - and built it himself. When he did need to call someone in for a specific job like laying the foundation, he sat with them and watched so that, next time, he'd be able to do it himself (and sometimes he'd even think, "I could do a better job myself!").

The same thing happened in those corporate training courses. David would sit there thinking, "I don't need to pay $600 to learn this. I could pick it up from a book." Only there weren't any books available. So, as a side gig, he started writing books on customer service and set up a website.

Back then, getting noticed online was simple: you gave the site a relevant name, put a few keywords on it, and Google would put you on the front page (these days, online business takes more skill, but nothing you can't learn if you're willing to put in the time and do the work).

He also had plenty of time to write in the evenings while he was attending the courses. Stuck in a hotel room with nothing else to do, he'd finish 10-15 pages every night, and after a week or two, he'd have completed a book.

That was David's business until 2015. Then, over time, he added more books, and related products that he sold to companies, schools, and universities. He even ended up teaching customer service at one of the companies he'd worked for. It was a simple and effective side hustle that made him up to a thousand dollars a month with minimal effort.

It's worth saying again that this has never been David's full-time job. That's a key point about being an info publisher: you can treat it as your primary source of income, or you can put in less effort and use it to make some extra money on the side. And as you'll see in many of the chapters in this book, there are times when that second income is incredibly useful.

David retired a few years ago, and he's been able to put more time into the business - at least until he became a grandfather and started spending time babysitting. That's another thing to bear in mind: the flexibility that comes with running a business. Unlike a job, you can put as much (or as little) time into info publishing as you need or want. You can jump in if you have plenty of time on your hands, and when things get busier - or a new commitment like kids or grandkids comes along - you can slow down.

Challenges

In the early days, David was shipping physical products: people would order a program on the site, and he'd print, bind, and ship it to them. Later, he switched to digital delivery, which took away the hassle of physical product fulfillment, but it came at a price.

As setting up a digital business became easier, a flood of new competitors came into the market - including major companies. David even found himself up against Disney (and their corporate marketing budgets) in a battle he couldn't win.

Even though his site was dedicated to customer service, sites about entirely unrelated topics started outranking him on Google. What was happening was that search engines were becoming more about advertising and less about content, and site owners were gaming the system. David refused to follow suit.

He wasn't interested in hacks and shortcuts or filling the site with spammy backlinks - that's not the foundation of a solid business built to last. So instead, he decided to diversify.

One of the significant advantages of being an info publisher is that, because you're creating your own products and content, you can easily pivot or expand into new areas. David saw an opportunity and decided to leverage his own experience to teach people how to launch information products.

A big struggle for David has been that, as much as he loves writing and creating content, marketing leaves him cold. But, like any good business owner, he's made sure to educate himself about it because, without good marketing, a business will die.

I signed up for Nick's Serious About Six Figures program, and my head got so full of ideas and insights that I had to keep a notebook on the nightstand because I'd wake up in the middle of the night thinking of new ways to promote the business, and I didn't want to forget anything! **Dave Greis**

One of David's personal challenges is that, because he loves creating content so much, it can take over. He'll sit down at the computer to work, and before he knows it, his wife is yelling that it's dinner time and he should be taking a break - something that will be familiar to many people who are lucky enough to be in business doing what they love.

So, he's found that the best way to work for him is to dedicate time to the other aspects of the business, not just on a daily basis but also when he's planning his year. For example, he has a new product launch coming up in a few weeks, and once it's done, he'll take six months off from product creation entirely and focus on marketing. The critical thing for David is that, as much as he may prefer just writing, he enjoys his business overall. Indeed, he says that the day he stops enjoying it, he'll stop doing it.

Hands-On Or Hands-Off?

Another great aspect of an info publishing business is that you can be as hands-on or hands-off as you like. So, even when David eventually stops working on the business, it won't necessarily mean he'll stop making money.

It's like being a performer. Elton John writes a song once, records it, and releases it. Then, for years after, every time someone plays it on iTunes, Spotify, or a radio station, he gets paid, even when he's asleep.

It's the same in info publishing. Take the customer service site, for example. For the last few years, David hasn't done anything to update or promote it. But it still delivers sales on autopilot. And even if it's only a hundred dollars a month, it's money he hasn't had to work for. And every part of David's business works the same way.

We said earlier that, rather than get bogged down in "hacking" the Google algorithm or looking for "silver bullets," he'd rather look for new markets to serve, and get in ahead of the competition. His approach to that is simple: he'll watch what's trending, and if a subject is interesting, he'll research it, write a book, and publish it on Amazon.

Even so, that doesn't mean David has to be constantly looking for the "next big thing": the last time he published a new book was two years ago, but every month a few hundred dollars get auto deposited in his account. And over time, those hundreds of dollars add up to thousands or tens of thousands of dollars.

David does a lot of his research for new books and products on his laptop in the evening in front of the TV, and many of his sales pages have been created while the news is on. For writing, he spends a couple of hours a day at the main computer in his home office - especially on days when the weather is miserable or his wife has gone out for the afternoon.

"Easy" Money?

Spending time with his grandchildren is a priority for David - he and his wife look after them three days a week. So. It's important to him that the business never become a full-time commitment. In total, he spends about 20 hours a week working, and he always leaves the laptop at home when they're on vacation (though, of course, the business continues to make money even when he's not actively working on it).

Even when all David had on the site was his books, the customer service website made $1,000 a month. But to monetize it further, he started emailing his list of buyers regularly to ask what other topics they were interested in. He'd get 20-30 replies each time, and if three or four people mentioned the same thing, that would be his next book.

Ironically, two of his best-performing books had nothing to do with customer service. For Valentine's Day one year, David decided - just to see if it would work - to write a book on how to be a better husband, and another on how to be a better wife. Most of the year, they get no sales. But every January, like clockwork, sales soar. People buy them as a joke gift for their spouse - not that David cares why people buy his books, as long as they keep buying!

Writing and publishing a book can seem a daunting prospect for many people. Like anything, the first time you do it can be a challenge, but once you've figured it out and learned the process, it becomes easy.

Getting Help

Over the years, David has not been afraid to seek help when needed. He joined a couple of high-ticket coaching programs, but they didn't give him what he needed. One of the programs was consistently late releasing lessons, and by the end of the year, they'd only delivered half the content. The other program had regular teaching calls and group coaching sessions, but David always felt something was missing.

Then, one day, David was talking to another info publisher, Steven Alvey, and the name "Nick James" came up. Steven is someone David trusts and admires, and he thought, "If Steven is recommending Nick's program, he must think this is good." So, David joined my Serious About Six Figures program. He ended up emailing Steven personally to thank him for the recommendation.

"(Nick) taught me a different way of looking at things, like not to sell cheap products, but to sell high quality ones. The lessons were very, very good. But what blew me away was Nick himself. I'd ask a question in the group, and he would say, 'Let's get on Zoom and discuss this.'

"I'd never had that level of support before. Here was someone getting on Zoom with me one-on-one and telling me, 'You should do X, and then do Y. Don't do Z.'" **Dave Greis**

One of the biggest things David got from the program was to stop undervaluing his work. It's a mistake I see way too many info publishers making - they assume it's easier to sell cheap products, so they'll make more money.

Let's unpack that for a moment. First, while it may appear easier, in reality, it takes almost as much work to get someone to buy a $10 or $100 product as it does to sell them a $1,000 product. And just because you price a product at $10 instead of $1,000, that doesn't mean you'll sell a hundred times as many, so you end up making a lot less money in total.

Second, when you sell cheap products, guess what kinds of customers you attract: cheap customers who don't value what they're buying and probably won't even open it, let alone apply it. Worse, those customers only bought from you because the price was so low. So, if someone buys a $5 product from you, it's hard to get them to buy a $50 or a $200 product later.

Put it another way: would you rather work hard to sell 100 copies of a $9 product and make $900, or work a little less hard, sell 25 copies for $100, and make $2,500 and fill your list with $100 buyers instead of $9 buyers?

"With Nick's guidance, I took a front-end product I'd been selling for $17, bundled some other stuff with it, and I ended up selling 50 copies at $150 each!" **Dave Greis**

A Hobby That Pays You Money!

David has always focused on businesses with low startup costs. What attracted him to working online was that the only fixed cost he had to commit to was web hosting. So, if a business failed, he might lose a few hundred dollars in the first year, but he would never have to go to his wife and say he'd lost thousands.

Many people, when they retire, take up a hobby that ends up costing them thousands of dollars. For example, if you take up golf, you need to buy equipment, join a club, pay green fees, drive to tournaments or matches, and so on.

David is lucky that he has found a way to make his hobby - writing - pay him instead. So, something you might want to think about is how you could turn an existing hobby, interest, or passion into an income by becoming an info publisher.

An Easy Retirement

As we've seen multiple times in this chapter, David's business is not a full-time gig designed to bring in a full-time salary. He freely admits he could make more money if he wanted to, but he enjoys the flexibility this work gives him.

And every dollar he makes is a dollar he and his wife don't have to take out of their retirement accounts. In fact, they have more money now than when he retired three years ago.

Many people worry about retirement. They know they haven't put enough money aside, so either they will have to change their lifestyle, or they're going to run out of cash. However, that's not a worry for David and his wife.

Throughout the years that he was doing this alongside a regular job, they were able to save and invest much more than if they hadn't had that side income.

And that's the big impact the business has had on his life: security. If David decided to pack up and stop tomorrow, he and his wife wouldn't have to change their lifestyle.

If one of their children suddenly needed a lump sum of money for something, he could give it to them. David even heard that thanks to new medical advances, people will soon be able to live until they're 130. So, he's already planning new books!

David's Advice

If you're on the fence about starting your own info publishing business and leaving the nine-to-five rat race, do what David did: start your business while you still have a full-time job.

Face your struggles and learn from them. Be open-minded and understand that you're not perfect (and you don't have to be). This is your opportunity to take control and responsibility for your own life. Nothing that happens to you is anyone else's fault. "They" don't do anything to you; you do it to yourself through the choices you make. And even if you've made bad choices in the past, accept them, and make a commitment now that you won't make the same mistakes again.

You can start an online business with next to no risk, and unless you're homeless, you can always find a few dollars to start doing something, whether it be affiliate marketing, creating your own product, or writing a book. Whatever it is, start it now as a side hustle, build it up, and get the income you need.

That way, if one day you can't stand your job anymore, you can go in and tell your boss to go to hell, knowing that you'll have a soft landing. Or, if something like COVID comes along and you lose your job, you can feel safe knowing you have a backup strategy already up and running and making money.

.

CHAPTER 6

Dr. Fred Ray Lybrand, Jr.

D r. Fred Ray Lybrand, Jr. (I'll just refer to him as "Fred" from now on!), from San Antonio, TX, happily admits that, over the years, he has "plundered" (taken the best bits from) over 5,000 books and spent nearly $80,000 trying to understand the constantly evolving beast that is marketing - figuring out how to "play the game" and keeping up with the latest ways to meet potential clients' wants and needs.

Along the way, someone recommended my book *Six-Figures a Year in Info Publishing* to Fred, and he was hooked. He has read it twice, even though he's a busy guy. Despite being "retired," he is the COO of a startup that delivers physical therapy digitally and recently finished his tenth book.

That's all in addition to running an online business that offers twelve courses for parents who want to homeschool their children, a related YouTube channel, and several Facebook groups.

Fred is an excellent example of someone who has monetized his life experience. He and his wife, Jody, homeschooled all five of their children, preparing them to be independent, fully engaged adults. Fred understood that when it came to homeschooling his children, he couldn't compete with schools on their terms: he didn't have the resources, additional teaching staff, or breadth of curriculum they do. So, he focused on what he could excel at: teaching his children how to learn (so they could pick up any skill they needed at any time in life) and how to be entrepreneurial. As a result, their children all paid their own way through college, and today they are employed and married with children of their own (Fred has eight grandchildren, with a ninth on the way!), and they are all active in their communities.

Amazingly, Fred and his wife achieved all that in just 30 minutes a day, acting as what he calls "Chief Learning Officers," making sure the children were doing what needed to be done. The rest of the time, the kids taught themselves. That philosophy underpins what Fred teaches his clients today through his business. And, as you can imagine, it's a business that did very well during the pandemic.

Fred's business teaches homeschoolers the soft skills they need to transfer to their children, including focus, goal setting, time management, relationships, communication, memory, writing, reading, problem-solving, parenting, and emotions. Customers can buy courses individually, or they can access everything at a deeply discounted rate.

And here's something interesting about Fred's programs. The reality is that anyone could use what he teaches - these are life skills that apply everywhere and to everybody. But focusing his attention on a narrow niche allows Fred to have much more compelling conversations with potential buyers and makes the offer much more attractive to his target audience than if he simply pitched it as soft skills training.

Fred's mailing list has 7,000 subscribers, and 80% have bought at least one of his courses. Much of his lead generation is driven by his books. He has sold at least 15,000 copies of The Absolute Quickest Way to Help Your Child Change, and he has a book about writing that he uses for lead generation for his writing course. His new book, Independent Homeschool, will also be a lead generation tool but takes a broader approach, explaining each of the available programs, with links to the relevant sales pages.

The Power Of Writing

They say everyone has at least one book in them. As we saw above, however, Fred has written ten. Interestingly, even though he studied English literature and communication, he was terrified of writing. To get past his blocks and overcome that fear, Fred focused on the simple idea that if you don't have anything worthwhile to say, there's no point in writing a book. But, if you do have something valuable to share, getting that information out to people who need it is the most important thing.

> *Anything worth saying is worth saying poorly.*
> ***Fred Ray Lybrand***

If you focus on the value of what you have to say rather than obsessing about how to say it, you don't have to start with great. Instead, give yourself permission to write something that is not perfect right away. You can always get help later to polish what you've written, but you can't polish what's still in your head and hasn't made it onto the page.

Getting Started Online

Fred first got into online business in 2005. The family had just moved to a new city, and he launched it as a family project, paying his 16-year-old son to help him in the new venture. Above all, Fred wanted to model entrepreneurship for his children and give them a vehicle for experiencing the emotions that go with running your own business.

Fred's first product was the writing course. And, like all the best business ideas, it was inspired by his own frustrations. He wasn't happy with any of the writing courses available at the time. So, he developed his own approach, initially just for use with his family. As he started to teach his children, however, he spotted an opportunity: parents happily pay for a private violin or piano tutor for their child, so why not a writing tutor?

Fred started with ten students in his home at a fee of just $10 a month each for four months of lessons. It wasn't much, but it gave the family a little extra spending money. Over time, he refined the content, then ran a seminar (which he recorded - a great way to create a product, by the way) and put together a workbook. Finally, he turned it into an online program, and it grew from there.

Before going online, Fred already had a busy life. In addition to homeschooling his five children, he was a full-time pastor. The family wasn't poor, but he couldn't just go out and buy whatever he wanted. The online business gave the family a slush fund for things beyond the essentials. For example, Fred has always been an avid learner, but he lacked the resources to go out and learn whatever he wanted. Now, he could reinvest his income into courses on marketing or whatever he wanted. It gave him freedom and flexibility to pursue the things he cared about.

The Biggest Lesson Fred Needed To Learn

As a pastor, one of Fred's biggest struggles was that he had spent 25 years giving away his time, energy, and knowledge for free. Suddenly, he had to switch to charging for those things.

It took some time until Fred finally understood the value of what he was offering. The lesson he had to learn was that when you put out information that's helpful to people, they're happy to pay for it. So, you're doing them a favor by not keeping what you know to yourself. And when you charge for it, they tend to value it more, so they'll actually apply what you're teaching them.

For example, as a pastor, Fred did couples coaching for free. Today (he retired from the ministry in 2010), he charges for it, and he's found that couples that don't pay for the coaching don't work on their relationship, while those who pay do work on it.

Even if you're not a pastor, it can be difficult to transition to charging for something - especially if you're turning a hobby or a passion into a business. But at some point, you need to decide: Is this a hobby or a business?

Either answer is OK, but you need to choose. And if it's a business, then it has to make money. As an entrepreneur, you need to get paid so you can put food on the table, do the things you want, and contribute in ways you otherwise couldn't. Money is simply a way to measure value and circulate it. When you get money, you can choose the most valuable ways to use it, whether that's buying things, doing philanthropic projects, or setting it aside for the future.

That leads into another common challenge that Fred had to deal with: how much to charge. He quickly realized that there is no "right" price. Whether he felt he was charging a lot or a little, there would be some people who complained his information should be free and others who couldn't get enough of what he was offering and would end up buying the same product twice.

Your price should be dictated by two things: what the market will bear and what you are comfortable charging. You have to believe in the value of what you're selling (and if you don't, why are you selling it?). If your personal sense of the value of your product aligns with what the market thinks it is worth, you're in good shape.

Finally, you'll have to be guided by your own level of productivity and how much you want to make: do you sell one product at a high price or many smaller products for lower prices? You may have to experiment to find the right balance, but eventually, you will find the right price point for what you are offering.

Going "All-In"

Fred loved being a minister, but over time it started to get predictable, and there was a lot more he wanted to do and explore in life. Eventually, he reached a point where it was time to throw caution to the wind and throw himself into the business.

Unlike many entrepreneurs, he didn't have a Plan B - Fred has always believed that the problem with having a fallback plan is that, if it's there, you'll end up taking it. After all, Olympians don't have a Plan B: they are there to win the Gold.

Of course, you need to be smart and act responsibly; you need to take care of yourself and your family. But whether you have a Plan B or not, at some point, you will have to push beyond your comfort zone. You'll reach a point where you don't have everything figured out, and things aren't safe and guaranteed. It's like getting married: however in love you are, you don't know exactly what you're getting into, but you decide the risk is worth taking.

Wherever you are in your life right now, at some point, you reach what Fred calls 'profound dissatisfaction' with how things are, and you finally say to yourself, "I'm not doing this anymore. I am going to step out. If I fail, I fail, and if I win, I win."

That's the point where you have to focus on action, let go of the outcome, and see how things develop. Stop worrying about what may or may not happen in the future. We have no way of predicting future events, but too many people let their fears about what might go wrong dictate their actions. When you let go of the future, it frees you up to try things now. When Fred writes a headline and some sales copy, tries a new ad, or creates a new product, he doesn't know whether it will work. But if he let his fears that people might not buy stop him from launching anything new, he'd have no business. The reality is there are no guarantees, and the only way to avoid failure is to avoid action.

Just go ahead and do your stuff. Your audience will grow, and because they're connecting with the real you, they'll love you all the more.

Fred Ray Lybrand

The Power Of Coaching

While, as we said above, Olympians don't have a Plan B, what they do have is a great coach at their side. Fred is a coach, helping clients through his courses, books, and in person. However, having the right coaches has also been critical to his success. And the important word there is "right": at times, Fred has worked with coaches who weren't right and became a distraction.

> *"It's hard to think crooked and walk straight. Your thoughts give rise to your actions. So, if the way you think about business is wrong, you will fail. It's like being in a dark room and imagining the furniture is arranged one way when really, it's all in completely different places. All that happens is you stumble around in the dark until you eventually fall over. But once you understand how to think about your business, the next steps are obvious."*
> **Fred Ray Lybrand**

Fred joined my program Serious About Six Figures because he loves to learn from coaches who have already done what he's trying to do and can share their hard-learned lessons and point out what works and what doesn't.

> *"It's really hard to read the label from inside the bottle (or if you don't know how to read!). So, you need someone standing outside, looking at things objectively and reading the label to you - and for me, that someone is Nick James."* **Fred Ray Lybrand**

You're Never Too Old (Or Too Young)

One of the biggest factors that holds people back from starting a business is age: some think they're too old, others too young. To Fred, that idea is nonsense. He started his business in his 40s and he's now 63. In that time, no client has ever asked him his age. If what you are offering is valuable, no one cares how old (or young) you are.

In fact, business has become more fun as Fred ages because he has grown in confidence and perceived authority. Also, as he gets older, he worries less about what people think and feels more comfortable telling them hard truths.

So, if you tell Fred that you're too old or young to start your business, he'll reply by asking, "How do you know? And what if you're wrong?" Say you think you're too young and you want to wait until you're 'old enough' (whatever that means!). If you're wrong, you'll have wasted years when you could have been growing your business. And if you think you're too old and you've missed the boat, so you never start your business, you'll be missing out on a wonderful opportunity. As Fred likes to point out, Cervantes, the author of Don Quixote, started writing in his 50s. And Colonel Sanders was in his 60s when he created the recipe for Kentucky Fried Chicken.

> *"I get insights now at 63, and I think, 'Gosh, I wish I'd known that 20 years ago. But I'm so glad I didn't wait until I'm 80 to learn it!' So whatever age you are, just go for it."* **Fred Ray Lybrand**

Retirement Is Not the End

If you've just retired, there is no better time to take the leap of faith and start your business. Start by rethinking your idea of retirement. Think about what you want to accomplish in the next phase of your life. What is your big vision? What would you like to do that will allow you to lie on your death bed and think, 'Wow, I'm glad I did that!'?

> *"Too many people reach retirement and head for the bench. They watch TV, go for a walk, read a little - they fill their day, but they do nothing with their life. They just "exist. What a waste! You finally got mature enough to handle a lot of stuff emotionally and practically, and you chose that moment to get out of the game? Why not take all you've learned and experienced, and be generous to other people? It's time to share what you know, not keep it to yourself and take it to the grave."* **Fred Ray Lybrand**

Facing The Challenges

In many ways, business is like making friends. Do you focus on trying to win over people who don't like you and keep telling you to go away? Or do you pay attention to the people who enjoy being with you and spend time with them instead? One of the most critical lessons Fred has learned - and it took him until the age of

50 to finally get it - is that no matter what you do, one third of people will love you, one third will hate you, and one third won't care either way about you. Learn to live with that and accept that you can't get everyone to be a raving fan. Instead, put your energy and motivation into going above and beyond to deliver value for the people who are your biggest supporters and ignore the rest.

When he started, Fred stressed out whenever someone unsubscribed from his mailing list. So, he would print out their details and keep them all in a folder. After doing that for a whole year, he realized he had no idea why he was doing it or what he was going to do with the folder. From then on, he reorganized his business around the people who appreciated him and that he could really help, rather than those who didn't like him or disagreed with what he was teaching.

Part of the reason why entrepreneurs hate seeing people unsubscribe is that when someone says they don't want to be on your list anymore, it feels like they're rejecting you as a person. One of the most important lessons you need to learn is how to deal with rejection and stop taking everything personally. Your business isn't about you; it's about your clients. Fred had to learn to focus on the kids who were going to learn to write and the families learning to deal with emotions, and on teaching kids how to soothe themselves and be calm, not chaotic.

Of course, the flip side is that when a client tells you about the difference your program has made in their life, you need to accept it's not about you either: you weren't there. The change happened because of the information you shared. And that's a beautiful thing because, one day, when you're no longer here, that information will still exist, and it will still be changing lives.

A Family Business

So far, we've focused on Fred in this chapter, but his wife, Jody, is very much a part of the business. She writes books and creates content, too; when a client needs coaching or counseling, Jody will often be the one who speaks to them; and for the YouTube channel, Fred and Jody interview guests together.

It wasn't always that way, and in the early years, Jody resisted simply because she's the more practical and conservative of the two. But as she watched Fred's entrepreneurialism grow, she reached a point where she said, "You know, I've just realized that you'll figure out a way to take care of us."

From that point, Jody has been fully supportive. She's still the voice of calm and reason when Fred wants to take a big risk - like putting the business into debt - but one thing is guaranteed to keep her on-side: thanks to their business, the couple now has enough money in the bank to meet their financial commitments for 18 months even if everything disappeared and the money stopped coming in. In a world where 54% of families live paycheck to paycheck, that's a wonderful position to be in.

Of all that he has achieved, however, what makes Fred proudest is seeing the principles he has been teaching work in the real world. Recently, Fred got a letter from a client whose son is 18 and has Asperger's. She was homeschooling their other child, and the 18-year-old would listen to the recordings while his sibling was learning. One day, he came home and said he'd got a job at Walmart. It turned out he'd heard Fred's goal-setting video and set himself an objective to get employment. Then he created a plan and implemented it.

Advice If You're Considering Starting an Info Publishing Business

As an info publisher, you have great power to impact people's lives, and that impact starts inside you. So, you have to make it real in your own life first. Fred didn't settle on teaching homeschooling just because it was a way to make money, and he wasn't sending his children out to school while teaching the power of homeschooling.

If you're selling supplements but not using them, teaching a diet regime you don't follow, or doing anything incongruent with your business, it will catch up with you.

So, whatever you do, do it with integrity. When you talk about it, teach it, and build products, that integrity and authenticity will carry you through whatever comes your way. And, because you're a true believer, you'll attract other true believers who take what you teach to heart and use it to improve their lives.

Nick James combines two important qualities. You'll listen to him, and he'll give you insights. And you'll go, "Aha! This is what I've been looking for." But there's another practical side we miss, because a lot of what Nick says will remind you of something you already knew, but you'd forgotten to implement.

Putting together new information with what you already know but haven't done anything with is what gives you a complete strategy for building an online business. I'd be shocked if you were disappointed working with Nick, and I'd be shocked if you're the same person six months later.

Fred Ray Lybrand

CHAPTER 7

James Neville-Taylor

James Neville-Taylor lives in the UK but loves to travel, so info publishing is the perfect career, giving him the flexibility to work from anywhere in the world (when we spoke to him for this book, he was in Florida). As you'll read in this chapter, however, James is also great proof that it doesn't matter what your background is, or what challenges you've faced in the past; what's important is what you do to move forward.

James is a firm believer in the affiliate marketing business model, especially for promoting continuity programs and memberships where you make the sale once, and then you get paid over and over again for the lifetime of the buyer. And because you're promoting someone else's products, you avoid the technical hassles of creating the product, and the product publisher is responsible for support, not you.

Using that strategy, James has built a seven-figure affiliate marketing business, and much of that income is recurring. As an affiliate marketer, he is often at the top of leaderboards. But he doesn't just promote anything that will make money: he has to believe in a product before he will put his name next to it.

That's an important point if you want to become an affiliate marketer: your success will depend on whether your audience associates your name with quality products. So, you must safeguard the integrity of your personal brand above all else. One of the principal checks James puts in place is to buy a product himself before promoting it, and it's worth doing the same if affiliate marketing is the path you want to follow.

James also creates products of his own, ranging in price from $7 to $5,000 and beyond. But he didn't want to create yet another info product on how to do affiliate marketing. He wanted his program to be bigger and better. So, in addition to educational content, he used one of his favorite software-building platforms - Builderall - to create a platform that builds affiliate marketing campaigns automatically.

That's another great learning point to model in your business: as I said in the introduction to this book, when people hear the term "info publishing," they usually think of books and courses.

However, as you've seen in other chapters, adding software that automates or supports what the buyer is learning is an excellent way to add massive value to your offer.

When James launched the product, it was his first formal product launch (a process where you carry out specific activities to build excitement and demand ahead of releasing the product rather than simply hoping that "if you build it, they will come," as many marketers do). And it worked: James made $300,000 in sales in the first two weeks.

James's Story

Whether you're selling to individuals or to other businesses, people buy from people, and James's story is a big part of what connects his audience to him.

(Editor's note: what follows is an integral part of James's journey, but some readers may find it distressing. If you prefer, you can skip to the next heading.)

As a child, James was abused - physically, mentally, and sexually - by a succession of father figures. At 11, he was put into care, moving between 15 different care homes over the next four years. As a result, he never really got to know anyone or learned to trust - and sadly, some of the few people he did trust ended up betraying him.

It was a difficult time for him emotionally, and it didn't end even when he moved back in with his mother. Life hadn't prepared him to deal with the emotional and psychological realities of what he had been through.

So, he shut down, and in his twenties, he locked himself away, playing online video games all day and night as a way to lose himself in fantasy worlds and escape from the harshness, as he saw it, of the real world. In the virtual worlds he inhabited, James temporarily ceased to exist. And if he did go out into the "real" world with other people, he would seek refuge in alcohol.

The barriers James had put up kept him safe for a while, but eventually, the real world started to creep back in, and he stopped enjoying the games and other distractions. That was when he hit rock bottom, and in January 2017, he took an overdose that almost killed him. As tragic as that was, however, he sees it as the wake-up call he needed and the best thing that could have happened to him.

Getting Started Online

Suddenly, James realized how much time he had wasted and, more importantly, that no one was coming to save him. He stopped feeling sorry for himself and instead decided to sort himself out. He still couldn't look people in the eye or have a face-to-face conversation with someone, and the thought of getting a job in a store or a factory where he'd have to be around other people all day filled him with panic.

James was living on welfare and hated being so totally dependent on other people. He wanted - and needed - to prove to himself and to everyone around him that he could stand on his own two feet. So, he started looking online and redirected the same energy that had kept him in online games 16 hours a day into the world of internet marketing.

One of the first things he tried was setting up an online agency, but that meant getting on the phone with potential clients, which filled him with dread. The first time he booked a call, he spent a whole day preparing, trying to anticipate every possible question they might ask him and prepare answers.

He drank a dozen cups of coffee as he waited for the scheduled time. Finally, he picked up the phone and dialed. It rang, but no one picked up. He tried again ten minutes later, and again no one answered. Finally, the next day, the prospect sent a message to say something had come up. In the end, the call never happened, and all the prep work had been a waste of time.

Over the next six months, James tried other ways of getting started, but nothing worked. Then one day, he found an email in his inbox about a software platform called Builderall. Initially, James dismissed their marketing as hype, but when a second email came in, he decided to check it out. He loved it so much that he set up an affiliate account and started telling people about the software everywhere he could: in emails, on social media, and anywhere else he could think of.

The sad truth is that many people would have given up long before reaching that point. We live in a world obsessed with instant gratification, where six hours is too long to wait for a result, let alone six months. But James pushed through, and thanks to affiliate marketing, his first commission payment was for $1,000.

The day that money appeared in his account was inspirational. Finally, here was income he had earned for himself. It was something he could be proud of, and it gave him the belief he needed that he could make this work - a conviction he nurtures in his clients because it's the key to building a successful business.

The following month, James made another $1,000, then $2,000, and it kept growing. Less than a year after trying to take his own life, he was one of Builderall's top affiliates.

In the years since then, James's life has turned around massively. He has traveled to 15 different countries and experienced things he could never have imagined growing up.

James and I met at an event in Orlando, FL. I'd just finished speaking on stage, and he introduced himself to me in the lobby. In the bar later that day, we compared experiences of starting our online businesses and became friends. Since then, James has invested in several of my programs and products, including Six Figures A Year and our PLR newsletter, and always invests in any PLR or MRR we issue. For him, the biggest lesson he learned from working with us has been always to overdeliver.

> *I've been a subscriber of the PLR Newsletter for a long time now, and the value you get is insane. I think that Nick could (and probably should) charge two to four times more for the content and value. He's got a subscriber for life with the PLR newsletter.* **James Neville-Taylor**

At 60,000 subscribers, James's mailing list is large but not, by the standards of the info publishing industry, massive. Like many info publishers, he is working on being more consistent in communicating and building engagement. But that's another point worth noting: even though James hasn't put as much effort into engaging his list as he would like, he has still managed to build a seven-figure business.

Get Support

Growing a business on your own is a lot of work, especially when it's time to step up to another level. For James, a significant factor in scaling his business to seven figures was taking on other people to work for him. After launching his program, he started hiring contractors. However, one of the biggest factors in growing the business has been working with a coach. When James started, of course, he couldn't afford one. So, he had to figure everything out on his own.

> *"Sheer grit and determination can get you through the early stages, but to really take things to the next level, you need to invest in yourself and get a coach or a mentor. Things can go off the rails frighteningly easily if you don't have someone to guide and help you when things go wrong - and things will go wrong."* **James Neville-Taylor**

Like many of the info publishers in this book, another source of support for James has been the info publishing community itself. When he first started online, James was too anxious even to put up a profile picture on Facebook. He was so convinced he had nothing of value to say that all he did was share quotes and memes. Then he finally got the nerve to put up a profile picture and, guess what? He didn't die! And little by little, he started creating his own content to post.

Then, in October 2017, he was asked to speak on an online summit for Builderall's members. At first, he declined. He'd never created even a ten-second video, let alone a 45-minute presentation, and he was still struggling with his crushing fear of connecting with other people. But when he put the phone down, he remembered a quote from Richard Branson: When someone offers you an amazing opportunity, and you can't do it, say 'yes,' and learn how to do it later.

James realized this was an excellent opportunity to build his profile and catapult him into the spotlight. So, he called the summit organizers back and agreed to talk, even though he would only have two days to prepare. He went out the same day, bought a new mic and camera, wrote his presentation, and scripted it word-for-word.

On the day, disaster struck right from the start of his presentation. There was a problem with his setup, and the audience could barely hear him. For forty minutes, people were leaning into their computers, trying to hear what he had to say. It was only at the end of the session that James looked down and saw, to his horror, the red light on his mic that indicated he'd been muted the whole time - and he quickly turned a similar shade of red!

Instead of trying to bluff his way through and pretend it was a technical hitch, James took the mic off mute and admitted what had happened. That was the moment he realized he had found his tribe. Instead of laughing at him, everyone was supportive and caring.

Luckily, the summit wasn't live, and this had been a recording session. The only people watching and (barely) listening were the summit team, and they did their best to boost his confidence. And they invited him to rerecord his talk a couple of days later. That supportive, inspiring community turned what could have been a very negative experience into a positive one.

The highlight of James's career in info publishing came a year later, in October 2018 when he was asked to give a 15-minute speech to an audience of 100 people. He flew to Italy and spent the night before practicing in his hotel room for five hours.

It was the first time anyone had asked James to speak from the stage to a live audience, and just like the summit, it didn't start well. The first words out of his mouth were, "I've never spoken to more than five people before," and he had a notepad on stage which he kept checking as he presented.

But then he started to share his story. It was raw, and it was real. Even though his delivery was terrible, he got a standing ovation. It was a transformational moment that made him realize he truly could do anything. He wanted to cry, but at the same time, it felt like his heart would burst with joy and pride.

Take Action

When James first started, he stressed out over every detail. He would rewrite a post ten times, checking the spelling and grammar and going through it with a fine-tooth comb to make sure nothing could be taken the wrong way or out of context. A job that should take five minutes would take half an hour, and when he finally clicked 'Post,' it was terrifying. Fortunately, these days, James will write a post, put it up without even checking it, and see what happens.

Fear of putting themselves "out there" holds many people back for years as they wait for everything to be perfect. If that's you, James's advice is simple: just take action. We all worry more than we should about ourselves. Everything in our own life seems so much more important than it actually is, and when you realize that, it puts things into perspective. To quote the well-known book title, "Don't sweat the small stuff. And it's all small stuff."

Decent people are more worried about themselves than your silly little mistakes. Yes, there are trolls and idiots everywhere, but - as we also saw in Fred Ray Lybrand's chapter - who cares what the haters think? They're not the ones you should be paying attention to; focus instead on the people who like you and want to hear your message, because they'll forgive your mistakes and may even love you more because of those flaws - they just show that you're human too.

The key is to keep pushing ahead, even if the individual pushes aren't massive: a succession of baby steps will get you just as far as one giant leap. Putting up a profile picture was scary, but it was a step in the right direction. Speaking on the summit pushed James out of his comfort zone, but it was another step. His first live call with a group of clients was terrifying, but it moved him forward a little more. There's no way James could have stepped out onto a stage in front of an audience in 2017, but his actions leading up to the event in 2018 made that presentation just another step on his path. And because of it, two weeks later, he was in Germany, speaking to an even larger audience, and in Brazil a few months after that, presenting to 400 people.

As long as you are taking action, you'll keep moving forward. The moment you stop and try to stand still, you'll start going backward because the rest of the world is still moving, and they'll leave you behind. So, trust your judgment and push through. If you make a mistake, own it, apologize, and get over it (and yourself). That is what will skyrocket your success.
James Neville-Taylor

Whatever you need to do that terrifies you, figure out some baby steps to help you get there. If making a presentation to a group of people fills you with dread, start by recording some short videos - just you on your phone talking about something you've learned. You don't even need to post them at first if that's a step too far. Build your confidence little by little, and when you're ready, you can post stuff out to the world.

Life As a Seven-Figure Entrepreneur

James's success didn't happen overnight, but it didn't take decades, either. In just four years, he went from zero to seven figures. One of the biggest changes has been in how he treats himself; specifically, he has finally started treating himself properly.

He has also done something most people aren't willing to do when they start making lots of money: for the last few years, he has lived frugally in order to reinvest as much as possible back into the business and himself. He spends thousands of dollars every day on advertising to keep the business growing. And he invests in his own training and personal development to keep himself growing.

When your business first starts to grow, it's essential not to upgrade your life too fast. Most people in that situation will go out and buy new clothes, a new car, maybe even a new house. While it's good to enjoy your rewards, if you rush to fulfill your ambitions, you'll lose your edge. Once you have the new house and car, and the upgraded wardrobe, it's easy to get complacent. If you can resist that desire for instant gratification, it will keep you hungry, and you'll push for even more success.

Even when he started making $10,000 a month, James carried on living in a cold, damp, run-down house. He bought a tiny used Suzuki Swift for $300 that didn't even have power steering.

But as a result, today he has lots of money that he can take out and "play" with.

Entrepreneurship is not for everyone. It takes a lot of determination and effort to get to the equivalent of a good 9-to-5 salary. But if you want freedom, James is convinced that no other business model can compete with info publishing, especially affiliate marketing. If you're committed, determined, and want to make an impact and live a life of purpose, just get started. It won't happen overnight - it takes time - but it's worth it.

The 'laptop lifestyle' - traveling the world working wherever you want - is a bit of a cliché in the info publishing industry, but freedom was always part of James's plan. As long as he has a laptop and an internet connection, James can work anywhere, even on a beach in Mexico (which he has done!). Obviously, COVID made travel difficult for a while, but James started flying again as soon as possible. When we spoke to him in Orlando, it was just one stop on a personal-development trip that has taken him from Mexico to Texas and Florida. Yes, it's a cliché, but it's one that James is happy and thankful to enjoy.

CHAPTER 8

Jeremy Kennedy

Jeremy Kennedy from Arkansas in the US teaches entrepreneurs how to start or get more exposure for their business by taking their knowledge out of their heads and turning it into products and courses.

Jeremy started his company in 2012 and, throughout his online career, his watchword has been KISS: "Keep It Simple, Stupid." There's nothing wrong with having big dreams, but if those dreams get too complex, things get trickier.

So, Jeremy's business model is simple: he uses small information products to get people onto his list then puts bigger offers and affiliate offers in front of them. It all happens in three easy steps:

1. *Sell a small product.*
2. *Add the buyer to your mailing list.*
3. *Focus on helping them and finding more ways to deliver value.*

As uncomplicated as that model is, it has consistently generated multiple six-figure revenues year after year. Many small businesses fail in the first two years, and many more disappear by their fifth year, so making it past ten years shows just how powerful this business model is.

People are addicted to knowledge and information, so you can keep doing that, and you'll have customers for life. Because if someone is interested in a topic, they'll happily invest in college courses, coaching and consulting, books and ebooks, 30-day challenges, live events, information products, and anything else they can find. And they'll keep doing it time and again throughout their life: Jeremy has customers who bought his first ebook over ten years ago and are still buying his products today.

> *If you want a winning direction, go to Nick. I've been doing this for ten years, and he's the guy to go to. He will steer you right and show you how to make as much money as you want in this business.* **Jeremy Kennedy**

The Joy Of Info Publishing

Even when the COVID lockdowns began, business was better than ever for Jeremy. While most entrepreneurs were panicking about what would happen to their store or service business, Jeremy saw an upsurge in sales as people started spending more time online and took advantage of being stuck at home to re-educate themselves and think about their future

One of Jeremy's favorite aspects of info publishing is that when something unexpected happens in life - or even if you just want to take a break - you can step away from the business and still make money. There's no better feeling than spending a couple of days creating a new ebook or course, taking 15 minutes to write an email, sending it, and watching money come in for the rest of the day (and keep coming in over the weeks and months that follow).

The key is to build recurring revenue into your business: memberships or services that you sell once then people pay you for each month - that's when info publishing really replaces a regular job because you have a stable, predictable revenue that pays your monthly bills.

Starting The Business

Jeremy had always wanted to run a business but hadn't been able to figure out what it should be. Before starting in info publishing, he tried many jobs - everything from retail work to driving an 18-wheeler - until he ended up doing web design and stumbled into online marketing by chance. Like many people in the industry, he started as a 'consumer,' buying products and courses to learn how to escape the nine-to-five grind and make a living online. Then he realized that he needed to be the person selling the products, not buying them. Of course, as soon as he came to that realization, the first thing he did was buy another product, because now he had the "what," but he still needed the "how."

If I were starting again, the first person I'd go to now to learn how to run an info publishing business is Nick James. **Jeremy Kennedy**

Jeremy's first product was an ebook that took him less than a weekend to write, and he sold 20 copies at $15. It doesn't sound much, but it was the first time he'd made $300 in a single day.

So, he decided to do it again. He created another product, launched it - still with very little idea of what he was doing - and this time, he made thousands of dollars in sales.

Then he did was something that neither he nor I recommend you do until you've got a few successful launches under your belt: he quit his day job.

As it happens, things worked out for Jeremy. He was able to make enough to support his family, and he hasn't had to work for someone else ever again. However, as we've seen in other chapters, a major advantage of info publishing compared to other ways of making money is that you can run things in your spare time alongside a full-time job while you build a solid base. You can put in an hour or two every day - just remember to tell your family you mustn't be disturbed during that time. If you make a little progress every day, you'll be surprised how quickly you can accomplish something worthwhile.

That takes a lot of the risk out of getting started. As long as you haven't burned any bridges behind you, the worst that can happen if you fail is you'll end up back where you started, but at least you took a chance. And if it works out, you'll know your idea is viable and you can make money from it.

For Jeremy, taking the plunge gave him confidence, and at the back of his mind was the thought that he hated the job he was doing, so he wasn't losing much if he failed. Even though he does consider himself a risk-taker - after all, he quit his job cold-turkey to start the business - he tries only to take calculated risks with a strong possibility of a correspondingly big reward.

Support From Family and Friends

Having the support of the people around you is critical when you start your business. The last thing you need is friends and family saying you're crazy to try and that it'll never work, telling you stories they heard about people who tried to start a business and failed, or worse yet, reminding you of your own past failures or shortcomings.

Jeremy was fortunate that his then-wife was 100% supportive as he started his business. As for his friends and other family members, he doesn't remember anyone not being supportive for a very simple reason: he ignored anyone who wasn't fully on board with what he was doing. If someone said anything negative, his response was "I appreciate your feedback" - and in his head, he would add, "but you don't have a clue what you're talking about."

If you feel the need to be an entrepreneur in your bones, and you're passionate about what you're doing, it doesn't matter what anyone else says or thinks. So, if you're surrounded by doubters and naysayers, remember that they can't see the future. Just because they heard about something bad that happened to their neighbor's second cousin's brother-in-law doesn't mean it will happen to you. After all, imagine if, when you said to friends and family that you were going to take driving lessons, they'd told you about all the accidents they'd heard about and all the people who die in road accidents. Would you have canceled your driving lessons?

There's Always Something to Learn

Throughout your career, pivotal events will stand out in your memory, and I was surprised and honored to hear that for Jeremy, that moment was meeting me.

We were both attending a mastermind and the room was full of industry heavy hitters. Like many new marketers, Jeremy was suffering from imposter syndrome even though he'd already built a six-figure business. Joining that mastermind was a life-changing experience for him, however.

Ask any serious business owner, and they'll confirm that their most successful years are almost always the ones where they're in a mastermind, learning from their peers. When you belong to a mastermind, you can learn things completely outside your experience from people who are ahead of you in their journey but only too happy to share.

In this industry, there are only two real ways to move forward. Either you take the path of doing everything on your own and learning every lesson the hard (and often expensive and time-consuming) way, or you learn from people who have already done what you want to do.

One way to do that is by joining a mastermind. Another way, which Jeremy recommends because it can accelerate your progress even more, is to get a business coach or mentor. Having the right advisor can be the difference between success and failure. The key is to pick someone who has already achieved the kind of success, impact, and income you aspire to; someone who is ahead of you on your chosen path.

"You can only go so far on your own, and when you try, you'll always end up hitting a ceiling of some sort until someone comes along and shares some critical piece of information from their own experience. It might be one little sentence, but there have been times when a single sentence from someone like Nick moved the needle for me." **Jeremy Kennedy**

However successful you are in your business, there's always something you can learn. For example, Jeremy confided in me that one of the things I teach that had the most significant impact on him is how to use direct mail. I'm a great believer in putting things in envelopes and mailing them to your prospects, and I find it staggeringly stupid when a marketer says they don't believe in direct mail anymore and that electronic communication is the only way to go.

Let's do a little experiment. Open your inbox and look at how many unread emails you have. If you're like most people, there are probably thousands. In fact, some of my friends have tens of thousands of unread emails in their inbox. If you're good at keeping on top of things, there might only be a few hundred, but that probably means you delete most of the emails you get without reading them.

Now go wherever you keep your (physical) mail until it's opened. I doubt you have thousands of sealed envelopes piling up in the corner of your room.

Direct mail works *because* so many people have switched to email, SMS, and other electronic communication methods. So, when a real letter - or better yet, a package - arrives in the mail, it stands out and gets noticed.

Of course, you probably throw away lots of junk mail, but that's because it looks like a piece of marketing. The secret to getting your mail opened is to ensure it doesn't look like a bulk mailing: after all, if a hand-addressed envelope lands in your mailbox with an actual stamp (not a franking machine label), are you really going to throw it away unopened?

> *Nick is one of the best copywriters on the entire planet - and I've read copy from many good copywriters. Nick has some of the best sales copy in the world, and I genuinely love getting his letters in the mail. They're entertaining, funny, and informal, but they're also highly valuable.*
> **Jeremy Kennedy**

Jeremy loves getting my mail so much that it inspired him to use it in his own business, and he wanted to share a sneaky little secret for getting people's mailing addresses. When he promotes an affiliate offer, he'll give buyers a physical bonus that has to be mailed. That way, he has a reason to ask for their contact details - including a shipping address - even though they bought a product from someone else.

For example, on one occasion, he bought little commemorative coins on Amazon as his bonus. Sixty buyers used his affiliate link, so he asked for their address and sent out sixty coins, each with a letter promoting a $500 product of his own.

To make the letter stand out, Jeremy made it look handwritten. He wrote the master by hand and photocopied it (if your handwriting is not the best, you can always print a letter using one of the many handwritten fonts that you can pick up very cheaply or even for free).

He has been doing this for a while, and every time, he gets thank you emails from customers commenting that no one sends thoughtful handwritten letters anymore - even though the letter was photocopied!

And how did the mailing do? Three people took the $500 offer, and several more bought other mid-ticket offers. That's "free" money on top of the affiliate commissions he'd already earned from their original purchase - and all it cost him was 99c for the coin, plus the cost of the letter and a stamp. As we said right at the start of this chapter: Jeremy likes to keep things simple!

Life As An Info Publisher

As you've seen in other chapters, the benefits of running an info publishing business include not just being in control of your schedule, but also that once everything is up and running, it doesn't need much time from you to keep it going. On a typical day, Jeremy will get up, spend a few minutes writing an email to his list, and from that point, the rest of the day is his. He can decide whether to keep working or take the day off. If he's working on a new product, for example, he might work another hour or two, depending on when the launch is scheduled.

Another great aspect of this career is that if you've chosen the right niche, you'll be working with people you enjoy helping. It's fun spending your day talking to people who are interested in the same things as you. That's when it stops feeling like work.

Jeremy loves to travel, and he would rather spend money on experiences than things. So, you won't see a picture of him next to a Lamborghini or a Ferrari (he drives what he describes as "a fairly nice suburban"), but you will see photos of him enjoying himself in different locations.

On one trip, he wrote an email campaign from his hotel room in Panama City, and it paid for the whole trip. It's a formula he's repeated many times since then when he's traveling: each morning, he'll wake up 15 minutes early, send an email to his list promoting a new or existing product, and then enjoy the rest of the day.

Finally, whatever other people may tell you, running your own business is more secure than most jobs. If recent years have taught us anything, it's that there's no such thing as job security, and everything can be taken away virtually overnight. Having your own business, however, gives you control. When things are tight, you can create a new offer, send it out to your list, and start making sales.

Of course, running a. business isn't totally without risk: you could still go broke or, worse, bankrupt. Something could happen that takes away your business or your ability to make money - just ask all the marketers who were 'slapped' by Google a few years ago.

But at least you have control over what happens next - something very few employees can say.

"With so many people today living paycheck to paycheck, taking the leap to start an info-publishing business offers a way out. You can sell your life an hour at a time, eight hours a day for $20 an hour, or you can sell eight copies of a $20 product in five minutes with the potential to make unlimited income for the rest of your life." **Jeremy Kennedy**

Ultimately, it's about who gets to benefit from your hard work. As an employee, you're making money for someone else. And maybe your employer is a good person with a great business that helps people, and you love your work - but do you want to keep making money for them? Or do you want to focus on yourself, your family, and your financial security?

Jeremy knows that some people will choose the comfort of steady employment, and there's nothing wrong with that - not everyone wants to have a business. But he does point out that if you want ultimate freedom and the ability to make as much money as you want, then at some point, you are going to have to decide, "I'm doing this."

Just remember his earlier advice: if you already have a steady job, don't take unnecessary risks. You can start your business as a side hustle for an hour or two a day. That way, you don't have to quit your day job until you know precisely what you're doing and where the business is headed, and you can prove to yourself that it will work.

Too many people start their online business not knowing what they want to do: will they create info products, be an influencer, run a YouTube channel, or something else? Then they buy product after product that promises to share the secret of making money online. Don't do that. Instead, Jeremy's advice is to figure out what you want to do first, and then you can go all-in on that business model.

I've learned a lot from Nick, and I have to thank him for that. When I read Nick's story in his book, I could really relate to what he was saying and how you can drastically change your life just by sharing what you know through books and products. **Jeremy Kennedy**

CHAPTER 9

Michael Wilding

Michael Wilding, from London, England, is another entrepreneur who has had a rough journey, one that took him to some very dark places. But he's also very open about it because he knows how much better his life became when he came through that darkness.

Michael's primary business is a SAAS in the horse racing niche (which just shows you really can build an info publishing business on any topic!). He also works with seven- and eight-figure companies on scalability, company culture, and how to integrate technology to make the workplace more efficient.

That second niche came about by accident during a conversation over dinner at a conference.

A few people were discussing the challenges of integrating lots of new employees into a rapidly growing business. Michael happened to give his opinion, and someone at the table said, "You know what? That could work. Could you help us strategize it and implement it into my company?" That first client soon led to more work through word of mouth, and things continued to grow from there.

At 40, Michael has enjoyed great success, but it hasn't all been plain sailing. When he left school, he was supposed to go to university to study animation. However, two days before he was due to start, he changed his mind and went traveling for a couple of years instead.

Michael's family has a background in theatre, so when he got back, he enrolled in drama school. He loved his time there, and after graduating, he got an agent and became a working actor. At first, he got parts quickly and often had multiple roles at the same time. However, it didn't take long for Michael to realize that not all acting jobs are the same, and he hated some of the work he was getting.

But he also knew that, just like other industries, it was part of the job: if he wanted to get to the good stuff - the best roles, projects, clients, or whatever - he would have to pay his dues and put up with the bad along the way. Eventually, however, he got a job he hated so much that he decided to leave the theatre altogether.

Michael's girlfriend was obsessed with shoes, and he bet her that he could draw a better pair of shoes than she could. It worked out well because he had been missing the world of art, and he quickly discovered that not only was he good at drawing shoes but also, he enjoyed it. Initially, he was just doing it for fun, but one of the people who saw his sketches owned a company that made shoes for strippers and drag artists - shoes that don't only have to look fantastic, they have to be very well made. Michael became his unofficial apprentice and not long after, he was offered a place at the London College of Fashion. When he graduated, Michael ended up working for a high-end footwear designer, but left to set up his own custom shoe label.

Things went well until a recession hit the UK. Suddenly, it was bad PR for Michael's customers to be seen spending exorbitant amounts on luxury footwear while other people were struggling to pay their mortgages or buy food.

Sales dried up almost overnight. Michael tried switching to off-the-shelf shoes, but problems quickly started piling up. He didn't have funding to ramp up production for mass distribution, so he outsourced the manufacturing overseas. But the factories struggled to meet their delivery deadlines. It wasn't a fun time, and he had to shut the company down.

It was around this time that Michael discovered horse racing. Surprisingly, he isn't much of a gambler: he's quite risk-averse and prefers risks you can control (or at least understand). But he started to make a profit, and he got so good at it that he was approached to write a book and a blog, which is how Michael ended up in the digital world.

Michael had been producing content, but he wasn't selling anything. Occasionally, he'd promote something as an affiliate if a product creator approached him, but he wasn't actively going out and looking for products to sell.

However, running a website isn't free: there are regular costs that have to be met, and after a year, Michael realized he needed to monetize the site if only so it would break even. But it took another 18 months for inspiration to come to him.

Alongside running the site, Michael was still betting on horses, and he wondered how he could use technology to place bets faster. There was no existing software on the market, so he built it himself and started to sell it. (That's a great tip, by the way: if you're wondering what products to create, think about what's missing in the market that you wish someone else would make).

That created a fresh challenge for Michael because he'd never had to sell a product before. So, he reached out to someone with more experience and hired them to map out his launch. That was when the relationships he'd built promoting other product creators started to pay off: Michael was able to go back to them and invite them to be his JV partners.

Michael's first launch did six figures in six hours. But only because he had already spent two years building the relationships that made that launch work. Rapid results are possible in this industry, but sometimes it does come down to good old-fashioned hard work.

(That's another great tip: People just starting in the info publishing industry often ask me how they can find JV partners. One easy way is to pay it forward by promoting other people's products before you ask them to promote yours.)

The launch kickstarted Michael's online business. Very smartly, he sold a subscription rather than a one-off payment, which created recurring income. That should have taken away the pressure to run another launch immediately.

However, it was an annual subscription rather than monthly, which meant Michael still faced the challenge many product creators do: he had made a lot of money in a very short time, but now he would have to wait twelve months for his next big payday. Michael needed to create new, shorter timelines for the recurring payments, and he found a very clever way to do that (and correct another big mistake he'd made!).

During the launch, there had been no upsells. So, Michael quickly created two new products and offered them to everyone who had bought the software (while they were still excited!).

"I met Nick James at a Meetup. At that point, I knew nothing about marketing. I knew copywriting, and I could build a website, but I didn't really know about promotions as a whole, which is what Nick is great at. I read Nick's book, and I thought, 'Of course! Why have I not been doing this?' That's where I got the idea of making an upsell ." **Michael Wilding**

That's not the only time Michael has profited from implementing something he learned from me. In fact, a few years later, Michael launched an entire new business based on something he heard me say.

We were chatting at a Meetup, and Michael mentioned that he wanted to sell a physical product. I suggested a printed magazine and gave him advice on how to get it written and launched. Over the next six weeks, he built a basic website, wrote the sales copy, and got everything ready for the launch. To increase the perceived value of the offer, he implemented another of my ideas and formatted the content as a book rather than a magazine.

The offer was a $97-a-month subscription for which buyers got a new "book" each month. Within sixty days, Michael had over 100 subscribers - that's $10,000 coming in every month, like clockwork, without having to run a launch or drive traffic to a sales page. And it's not a complicated business model. In fact, running the business only took three or four days of work each month, and Michael did very little marketing for the program. Many sales were driven by referrals from existing subscribers, and he would email his list two or three times a week with an offer to subscribe, usually when the next edition was about to come out. The business grew over time, eventually stabilizing at around $20,000 per month. Michael ran that business for a couple of years then sold it.

(That's another tip to keep in mind: when you start a business, it doesn't have to be forever. You can launch it with the aim of exiting after a time by selling it. And having a proven, stable, recurring income massively increases the value of that business!)

Challenges Along the Way

One of my biggest motivations for writing this book is so that you can learn from the mistakes Michael and the others have made and take the lessons into your own business without having to go through the pain they did.

For example, as the business grew initially, Michael built a large team, which seems like a sensible thing to do in an expanding company. But it created a huge monthly salary bill. That was fine in months when there were lots of sales, but there were other months when things didn't go so well, and Michael worried about how he was going to be able to cover that payroll. So, these days, he deliberately keeps his team small; if he has an idea that would require hiring more people, he stops and asks himself why he wants to do it and whether it's absolutely necessary.

Over the years, Michael has launched many products and websites that didn't work. If it's obvious there's a problem while he and his team are still working on it, he will try to figure out precisely what's wrong: Is it traffic? Conversion? Retention? Is the message simply not resonating with the audience?

When something fails in your business, you may be able to pivot if you can pinpoint the exact point of failure. Sometimes, however, you only realize there's a problem when it's already too late. Then you need to think carefully about whether it makes sense to continue. Even if you've already built the product, remember you'll have to provide support, and there may be running costs. If it's a program, think about the time you will have to invest over the following months to keep it running. The key is not to take things personally. A failure just means you missed something or misread what your market wanted.

It's a tough decision, but there have been times when sales during a launch were so low that it wasn't worth going ahead, so Michael apologized and refunded everyone who had bought. In that situation, he'll often give them something else as a gift to keep the relationship going in the hope that they'll buy his next product or program.

One time, Michael spent $70,000 building a software product he never got to launch. As soon as he started testing it, he realized it was unusable. It was too complex for most people, and it would cost too much to redesign and rebuild. So, Michael drew a very painful line under it, learned his lessons, and moved on. At the end of the day, it doesn't matter how great a product is and how much time, money, or effort you put into developing it: if it doesn't meet your market's needs, it's useless.

Looking back on his failures, however, Michael realizes that most of them happened because he hadn't put enough money, time, or effort into marketing. And each time, it was because it was a project he'd started just for the money and his heart wasn't in it, which brings us back to the point you saw earlier, that you have to be doing things you love.

Michael's biggest struggle - and one which many entrepreneurs can relate to - is taking on too much. He loves a challenge, and when someone brings him one, he'll try to solve it. As a result, at one point, he was running four companies, building two houses, raising two young children with neurological issues, and supporting his partner. Then his father and grandfather both died, and he and his family moved in with his mother to support her, too. And all the while, Michael kept taking on more work and more responsibilities - often just to try to escape from everything else that was going on.

Michael didn't realize it, but he was approaching burnout. Like many people, he ignored the warning signs and tried to pretend everything was fine. One night, it all got too much, and he snapped. "Panic attack" sounds so minor - like being "a bit worried" or "a little overwhelmed." But it's not. Michael was reduced to a gibbering wreck, barely able to speak and unable to focus on anything except the growing feelings of panic.

Michael was lucky that when everything came to a head, he was surrounded by people who loved him. The support he got from everyone - his partner, both their mothers, other family members, and his friends - is the only thing that kept him out of hospital. An old friend came and sat with him for a week, talking and listening. He taught Michael meditation and other techniques to manage what was happening to him.

In the end, it took Michael a year to recover, and during that time, his mother kept the business going (although he's never quite worked out how!).

The Secret to Success

A lot of people get hung up on success. The key is to understand what that word means to you specifically. That sounds clichéd, but everyone has their own definition. And while money may be important, it isn't the only indicator of success.

For Michael, for example, success means being able to spend time with his young children (while they still want to spend time with their dad!). Like many of the info publishers in this book, his focus is on building a lifestyle business. Yes, he wants financial security and a home, but those things are secondary to him. If his business didn't allow him time for his family, it wouldn't matter if it was making millions - it would still be a failure.

So, when Michael takes on a new client, one of the first conversations he has with them is around boundaries. He sets a very clear expectation that he won't make himself available all day every day, and they are going to have to be flexible. The work will get done, but he's not going to sit online 24/7 just in case they want to talk to him. If a client pushes back, he knows they're not a good fit - and Michael has turned away some substantial companies because they wouldn't accommodate him on that.

Michael is also very strict about working only with clients who are coachable. It's not a case of "I'm always right, and you have to do everything I say," but they do have to take action. It sounds odd, but anyone who has ever offered coaching will tell you there are clients who pay you but don't listen to your advice unless it's what they were already thinking. That's another red flag for Michael. And the great thing about running your own business rather than being an employee is that you can be picky about the clients you work with. If something or someone doesn't feel right, you can walk away.

The Importance Of Outsourcing

As I say in *Six Figures a Year in Info Publishing*, there's a lot to do when starting your business. Some of those tasks will be things you enjoy, but not all of them. So, you need to be just as strict around what you allow onto your to-do list as you are about accepting potential clients.

Figure out what tasks you want to do and focus your energy on those. For the rest, decide how you will deal with them: will you assign them to a new or existing team member, outsource them, or can you simply let them go?

As an info entrepreneur, there's no rule that says you must do everything yourself, especially tasks you don't enjoy. If you force yourself, you'll usually end up doing it half-heartedly, and it'll take ten times longer than it should. Remember that you always have the choice to delegate a task and oversee it. That also means you don't have to know how to do everything in your business; you just need to know enough to tell whether someone is doing a good or a bad job.

Advice If You're Still on The Fence

As a business owner, you'll spend a lot of time working on your business, so it has to be something you enjoy. Otherwise, it'll just get harder and harder to motivate yourself and grow the business. You may even end up sabotaging yourself. After all, if you hate what you're doing, why would you put time and effort into growing it? That would just mean more work you don't enjoy!

One problem many business owners have is overthinking: it's easy to talk yourself out of an idea by coming up with all the ways it could fail or convince yourself that something is so simple it can't possibly work. In those situations, you need to trust the process and believe in yourself - many people have been down this path ahead of you and made it work.

Starting and running a business is a major undertaking, and if you treat it as one huge task that you need to get done, it's easy to scare yourself into thinking you'll never do it. Michael's advice is to take things one step at a time. It doesn't matter what your lifestyle is or how much time you can put into your business. Whether you're a single parent bringing up three kids or you have all the time in the world, pick one thing and finish it in whatever time you have available. Then move on to the next.

Nick is amazing at breaking things down into simple steps, so you don't even have to think. **Michael Wilding**

Focus on the progress you're making, not on where you think you should be, and break everything down into subtasks that match the available time. If you can set aside a whole day, pick something that will take a day to complete. If you only have an hour or two here and there, break things down into tasks that will take that long. That way, you can finish something and check it off your to-do list: that sense of completion is what will keep you motivated and making progress.

And, of course, another critical piece of advice from Michael is to get yourself a "Nick" of your own: a mentor who is looking at the big picture for you so that you don't have to worry about it and you can focus on the individual steps you need to take.

Work With the Skills You Have

Sometimes, we look at successful people and assume they had an easy ride; that everything just fell into place for them, and they had a grand master plan for their business. That's not Michael. From would-be art student to actor to shoe designer to horse racing blogger to management consultant, his career couldn't have been more random and haphazard if he'd planned it that way. And yet, he's been able to build a six-figure info publishing business.

At the same time, Michael does see a thread to everything he's done. Being an artist helps with the graphical aspects of working online. His acting background helps when it comes to creating videos and podcasts or presenting to a corporate audience. Working backstage on lighting and sound alongside his acting gave him confidence in working with technology.

Here's the point, though: none of those skills were about business or info publishing, but they were all transferable. And you, too, have transferable skills that may have nothing to do with this industry but will help you to get started.

CHAPTER 10

Mitali Deypurkaystha

Mitali Deypurkaystha has taken full advantage of the opportunity info publishing offers to live wherever you want. Originally from the UK, she lived for a few years in Thailand before returning to the UK with plans to move to Malaysia later.

Many people spend their lives consuming information - watching YouTube videos or reading free reports - without implementing. Mitali turns coaches, consultants, and business leaders from passive consumers of content into active creators by coaching them to write a book and helping them publish it.

This is not just about "being an author" and having a few copies of the book to give to friends and family. It's about creating a sales and marketing tool that provides real value to the reader - what many people refer to as "the ultimate business card." Also, it's essential to create a print book, not just an ebook. Nowadays, almost every online marketer has produced an ebook, so you need a print book to get true credibility and authority.

You may have been told that direct mail is dead, but as I've said elsewhere in this book, that's just not true. Mailing something in an envelope stands out and gets you noticed. That's why, when Mitali meets a potential client, she sends them a signed copy of her own book. It's an easy way to wow them, and you're not competing with thousands of emails and social media posts shouting, "Look at me! Buy my stuff!"

So far, Mitali has helped 23 professionals become published authors through a 90-day coaching program, and she's looking forward to ramping up her business. At the end of that process, her team of editors, designers, and typesetters take the manuscript the client has written and turn it into a polished book. To grow the business and allow her to work with more clients without adding more to her workload, Mitali also turned what she does into a prerecorded online program. She put an initial cohort of beta clients through the program, and now she's recruited affiliates to help her promote the program further.

If you're already a coach or consultant, turning what you would do one-on-one with clients into a prerecorded training program is an easy way to add info publishing to your existing business. It's also one of the best ways to scale an advisory business because it's not constrained by your availability, and you can work with people all over the world regardless of what time zone they're in.

Finding Inspiration

Mitali and I first met at a marketers' lunch in London, and she credits that meeting with inspiring her to turn her service into an asset. Here's the problem with selling any kind of service. Whether you're coaching, writing, running email or Facebook ads for other businesses, or whatever, you're just trading time for money. Essentially, you've given yourself a job, but with none of the safety nets that come with being an employee (at least in most developed countries). If you get sick, you stop earning. If you go on vacation, no one pays you. And you probably don't have a sales department or a marketing team finding customers for you: you have to go out and do that yourself, which is more time when you're not making money.

The only solution is to create assets in your business that will earn money for you without your direct intervention and that you can get paid for time and again: products, courses, software, and everything else you're reading about in this book.

> *"Nick has been an inspiration and was instrumental in expanding my mindset. When I started my business, it was just about not having to get up for work on a wet, dreary morning or having a boss shouting at me. That was all the motivation I needed to go it alone. But Nick was talking about creating 'assets' and 'positive cashflow' - so you have a business where you get paid first."*
> **Mitali Deypurkaystha**

People who sell their time are almost always paid after they've done the work - your hairdresser doesn't ask for payment until they've finished; even attorneys aren't paid until the case is settled. Mitali calls this situation "negative cash flow" because there's a time where you've done the work, but you haven't been paid yet, so you're at a disadvantage. It's almost inevitable in a "time for money" business because you don't know how much to charge until you know how many hours you have to work.

Positive cash flow is the opposite: you get paid first, so there's a time when you've got the money but haven't delivered anything yet. That's the norm when someone buys a product. For example, when you buy a pair of shoes, you can't take them out of the shop until you've paid for them. Likewise, you have to pay for a car before you drive it away, and you pay for your house before you move in. The seller gets the money upfront.

In Mitali's case, when someone signs on for a coaching package or her high-ticket done-for-you services, they pay in advance, and then she helps them get their book written and published. With her prerecorded video program, it's the same: a buyer signs up, and after they've paid, they get the login details.

A great advantage of being an info publisher is that the assets - products and programs - you create generate positive cash flow. And unlike a physical product that you can only sell once (then you have to make another one to sell), with an info product, you create it once and sell it repeatedly.

Getting Started

Mitali was a writer from a very early age. Growing up in England, her parents spoke Bengali at home. Aged four, she turned up for her first day of school expecting everyone else to speak the same language, but of course, they didn't. The other children didn't want to play with the "odd girl who spoke a funny language." Desperately unhappy, Mitali would sit alone in the corner of the classroom, where the class "library" (basically some picture books on a shelf) was kept. She picked up a book and started to flick through, and little by little, day by day, week by week, she picked up English by reading. That was the start of her life-long love of books.

Throughout childhood, Mitali followed the life plan her parents had laid out for her: becoming a doctor. However, she loved writing poems and stories, and when she was 16, a teacher entered one of her stories in a national competition, and it won. Mitali and 29 other prizewinners went to Edinburgh University for a summer camp to learn scriptwriting, and they got to co-write an episode of a TV soap.

That changed everything for Mitali. Suddenly she saw that this fun thing she liked to do on the side could be a way to make money. So, she changed the subjects she was studying at school. Out went Math and Science, and in came English. Two years later, against her parents' wishes, she went to university to study Media Studies instead of Medicine (her father didn't speak to her for the first six months!), and after she graduated, Mitali became a freelance journalist.

In 2013, Mitali stumbled into content writing almost by accident. A friend who was into online marketing told her about the changes Google had made to its search algorithm. The old practice of "keyword stuffing" (filling a page with random words designed to appeal to Google's bots) didn't work anymore - Google was prioritizing how long people spent on a site and how they consumed the content on the page. That meant website owners couldn't just hire someone for $5 from a 'cheap' country who barely spoke English anymore to create a thousand-word 'bot-friendly' article. Instead, they needed native English speakers who could write engaging articles to keep people on the site.

Mitali started working as a content writer for hire. However, she soon realized that copywriters - people who write sales pages - were able to charge a lot more than content creators, so she switched. A few years later, one of her copywriting clients asked if she could write a book for him. She'd never done it before, but she took a leap of faith, and she hasn't looked back.

The big change came in 2017 when I got her to start thinking in terms of assets and positive cash flow. Today, she has cut out a lot of the hard work of marketing by refusing to do anything that can't be repurposed. The core of her marketing is a weekly livestream. She sends a recording of that to a VA who transcribes it and turns it into 25 different pieces of content, including blog articles, social media posts, thumbnails, and shareable images.

> *"Finding ways to optimize your use of time is critical when you're running a business. Time is the one resource that is absolutely limited. You have a finite amount of time on this earth (and you never know when that time will be up). And you can't make more of it or get it back if you make the wrong decision. So, you always have to make the best possible use of the time you have."* **Mitali Deypurkaystha**

The Big Leap

Starting a new business is scary. Many people stay in a job - or start a business where they're just trading time for money - because it feels safe (even though it isn't). Better to have a "guaranteed" paycheck, they think, or at least know what you'll be invoicing this month than to risk spending time and money creating a product only to have it fail and end up with nothing. Most people would rather keep showing up and getting paid, even if they hate their job and it makes them miserable.

> *"I've never considered going back to being an employee. Being an info publisher is just too much fun. I feel totally in control of where my life is going. Yes, there are downsides, and the business could fall apart, but the way I see it, there's no such thing as a job for life anyway. You think a job gives you security, but it doesn't really."* **Mitali Deypurkaystha**

Becoming an info publisher does require a certain mindset - for starters, you have to think it's better to try and fail than never to try at all. As an entrepreneur, you must get used to failing and accept that not everything you do will work out. But you can't let that stop you from trying because you never know when an idea is going to turn into a six- or even seven-figure business.

Failure is inevitable, so as a business owner, you can't afford to be ashamed of it. Just know that each time you fail, you are learning and growing. Stop seeking approval from others, because sometimes that approval doesn't come. And learn to take criticism, because you'll quickly discover that there are many critics out there, and social media is full of trolls who have never created anything themselves but are only too happy to trash what other people are doing.

If that's not for you, that's fine. As Mitali sees it, the unhappiest people aren't the ones who stay stuck in a job they hate; it's the ones who set up a business because they desperately want to be entrepreneurs but don't have the right temperament. And just behind them are the ones who dream of starting a business "someday" but aren't willing to take the leap.

That's why a coach or mentor is vital for entrepreneurs. As you've already seen many times in this book, you need someone at your side who's been through the process of setting up their business successfully, made mistakes and learned from them, and is willing to share their hard-earned lessons with you and help you avoid expensive errors.

Affiliates Create Positive Cashflow

Info publishers mostly fall into two camps: either they're good at product creation, or they're masters of traffic generation. There's a third group, who are masters of both, but they are rare (and they're often the best coaches, of course!).

One of the first things you need to do is figure out which group you're in, which requires a lot of self-awareness and humility (many info publishers hate to admit that they're not marketing wizards). Mitali is clear in her own mind: she is a product creator. Split testing Facebook ads or trying to squeeze a few extra clicks out of Google Adsense leaves her cold.

In the long term, however, you will need both skills in your business to be successful as an info publisher. So, if you're not good at marketing, you have two options. Either you master those skills (which isn't always easy or cheap), or you find someone with those missing skills and hire them or partner with them.

Hiring a good traffic person can be expensive, so you probably don't want to start with that (Mitali has already decided to wait until her revenue hits seven figures before hiring someone). Instead, recruiting affiliates is a much more viable proposition for a new info publisher, and the best affiliates tend to be people who are great at driving traffic but hate creating products. That's why they became affiliate marketers in the first place.

Affiliate traffic is the best traffic you can get, and what could be better than letting other people send you traffic? That will free you up to focus on creating exceptional products your customers rave about. The key is to recognize that your affiliates are saving you from doing the work you hate - the traffic generation - so you need to be generous and reward them for the value they bring to your business.

And remember that you only pay your affiliates after you've been paid yourself, so affiliate marketing creates positive cash flow. That's not the case with most marketing. If, for example, you run ads on Facebook or Google, conversion is down to you: you have to pay for the leads they sent you, whether or not those leads turn into buyers. So, it's easy to end up with negative cash flow if there's a problem with your sales process.

If you're in the other group - someone who loves traffic generation but hates having to come up with ideas for new courses or products - then Mitali's advice is to focus on that. Put all your energy, time, and money into getting better at marketing, and forget about product creation. Then set yourself up as an affiliate marketer and find product creators who are struggling to get customers.

Giving Away Your Secret Sauce

Many of Mitali's clients are worried about putting "too much" information in their book. It's a common concern and not restricted to book writing: many professionals hesitate to create a product for the same reason. They're afraid no one will hire them if they can just buy a book or a product for a fraction of the cost.

Here's the truth, though. Information is free: you can find out almost anything you want in a few hours on Google or

YouTube. So, for most people, the problem is not lack of knowledge; it's lack of implementation and follow-through.

Often, when someone buys a book or product from you, they're checking you out to see whether they should work with you on a deeper basis (like a more advanced course or a program). What they want is, first, accountability - someone to make sure they implement. Second, they want someone to help them tailor and apply the advice to their specific circumstances. And third, they want someone to soothe them and support them when things aren't going right; to reassure them that they can get through it and that they'll recover.

So, don't be afraid to give everything away in your books, products, and webinars. Don't be one of those internet marketers who runs a two-hour webinar that's just an extended sales pitch. As an info publisher, putting real, valuable information into your products regardless of price point is what will get you five-star reviews and rave testimonials and will connect your audience to you and turn them into customers for life.

Will everyone buy a higher-level offer from you? No. Some people will make a small investment and never go further. Maybe they can't afford you, or they genuinely believe they can get everything they need from a $97 training course. Either way, they were never going to spend more anyway.

But if someone can't afford to work on higher-level programs with you, why would you begrudge them a chance to solve their problem? And maybe, when they're able to invest more, they'll come back, and because you helped them when they were down, they'll be even more eager to take the next step with you. Even if they don't, they will tell other people about you because you didn't hold back.

Making Positive Change

Many people fail in business because they have screwed-up ideas about money (think about some of the financial self-talk your parents probably programmed you with: "Money doesn't grow on trees," "Money is the root of all evil," or whatever). When you're selling products rather than services, it's too easy to let those negative thoughts take over and end up undercharging.

One of the most valuable things Mitali says she has learned from me is the simple reminder that as well as making a difference in the world, you need to eat and take care of yourself and your family. The two are not mutually exclusive: you can be doing good in the world and still make good money.

For example, Mitali has recently become more vocal about being vegan and positioned herself as a strong advocate for animal rights and ethical and sustainable practices. That has attracted other vegan entrepreneurs and sustainable entrepreneurs as her clients. And because of their shared worldview, they feel more closely connected to her, they're willing to pay more to support a business owner who shares their values, and they're more loyal and more likely to refer other conscious entrepreneurs to her.

If You're Still on The Fence

People find all sorts of ways to put off starting their business: they will spend days looking for just the right font, designing their business cards, or coming up with the perfect business name - anything to avoid taking the first step. Procrastination does not get you closer to your goals; it steals your time and sets you back even further.

> *"In high school, when it was time to study for my exams, I really didn't want to do it. To make myself feel better about not studying, I spent a day creating a beautiful hand-drawn, color-coded study schedule. By the time I finished, I was no closer to being ready for my exams, and I had even less time to prepare."*
> **Mitali Deypurkaystha**

The only thing stopping you is your own fear of failure. Being a business owner is scary because there's no one else you can blame - no boss or coworkers - when things go wrong, or your company fails. But the potential rewards, not only financially but in terms of your self-esteem and self-worth, far outweigh the discomfort of sticking your neck out.

If you know that info publishing is the right path for you, but you're hesitating, Mitali's advice is just to do it. Her first product sold for $17, and she gave *100%* commission to her affiliates. Why? Because she sold a $50 product on the back end, and that was where she made her money. But guess what: when you offer 100% commission, affiliates will bite your hand off to help you: what they see is that "magic" number, 100%, rather than the low price of the product you're selling. Mitali made about $7,000 from that first launch, which was a great start for someone who had not sold anything online before.

If you're already in business as a service provider, you probably have forms, questionnaires, surveys, or other collateral. You can repurpose those and start creating a low-cost program (say $47) with five videos of your best advice, along with some PDFs, forms, tools, and mindmaps. That becomes your first asset, and even if you only get a handful of buyers, you'll have paid back the effort you put into it. And then, you can start looking for other people to promote it for you in exchange for commission. Suddenly, you're an info publisher!

CHAPTER 11

Raj Sidhu

Raj Sidhu from the United Kingdom owns Pinnacle PLR, which provides private label products in various niches, including marketing and self-help. Even though Raj is only 31, he's been in this industry for over ten years. Like many people coming into the online business space, he dabbled in different ways to make money online, but by his own admission, he only got serious about the business two years ago when he started creating PLR.

Looking around the industry, Raj noticed that the people making the most money seemed to be product creators. Producing PLR for others to sell attracted Raj because it offered consistent income. Many product creators live from launch to launch. The problem, is it takes time to create a good product and release it, and when you follow the typical launch model, your cashflow tends to come in large 'lumps' with not much income in between (which is one reason why I'm such a fan of continuity programs where people pay you every month!).

Building The Business

Raj loves creating funnels and web pages, and he designs most of the graphics himself. If, like Raj, you're attracted to the technical and graphical side of working online, and you don't want to get caught up in running long-term coaching programs or workshops and events, PLR can be an excellent way into info publishing.

I often talk about the value of JVs in my books, and partnerships are Raj's primary traffic source. As you've seen many times in this book, JV traffic is highly targeted and converts well compared to other kinds of traffic. And as we saw in Mitali's chapter, relying on JVs and affiliates means that Raj hasn't had to learn the intricacies of digital marketing strategies like SEO or pay-per-click.

Interestingly, creating PLR means that Raj's business attracts three different audiences. First, he's built a network of experienced marketers with large lists who want a steady stream of new products they can offer to their community.

Second, he attracts new entrants to the information industry who want to start their business quickly and don't want to have to wait until they've created their own product. And finally, he attracts people who are interested in the content of the PLR for themselves.

Raj didn't have many contacts when he started, and his first few launches did OK, but they weren't spectacular. However, he knew this wasn't about running a single launch and getting rich overnight. And it's important to bear this in mind, whatever direction you want to take in info publishing: this is a long-term proposition. Getting known, building a brand, and establishing yourself takes time. So, your early launches will probably be small, but the more you do - and the more often you do them - the more confidence you'll get, and each launch will be better than the last.

From Part-Time to Full-Time

Many info publishers run their info publishing startup alongside a job in their early years until they feel ready to go all-in (as I've said in other chapters, that possibility is one of the big advantages of this industry). Others keep their full-time job going permanently and build an info publishing lifestyle business on the side to provide a better standard of living for themselves and their family than they could ever afford with just their day job. And finally, others keep a part-time job going as a safety net while letting their business be their main source of income.

Raj ran his online business alongside a full-time IT job until it got to the point where he was doing 18-hour days, and he knew he had to make a choice. Was he going to be an employee for the rest of his life or an entrepreneur?

Raj chose entrepreneurship but decided to wait until he had saved enough money to cover six months of living costs and pay the mortgage if things failed. And as luck would have it, just as he reached that point, an opportunity appeared. A member of his extended family owns a business that sells heating pumps. They needed someone to take care of their e-commerce platform, but only part-time. So, Raj quit his IT job and stepped in.

Being an info publisher gives Raj the flexibility (and the skills) to help his relative to grow their business. And because the job is only part-time, it also allows him to dedicate time to his own business. As a result, he's been able to get better organized and launch products more regularly, which has allowed him to make more money than he ever could as a full-time employee.

Like many of the successful info publishers featured in this book, Raj's advice to anyone considering a career in info publishing is to build your financial buffer while you're still in a full-time job. Put aside enough money to cover your expenses for at least six months, as he did. While you build up that reserve, dedicate your spare time to getting the business started - instead of wasting several hours every evening watching TV, use that time to create your first product and set up a web presence.

Raj was lucky that his wife has always been very supportive of his entrepreneurial ambitions. It helped that he took things gradually and made sure he had that safety net in place before quitting his job - if you're facing resistance at home to the idea of starting your own business, it can be very helpful to say, "I'm doing X, Y, and Z to make sure we'll be OK."

The Power Of Focus

If you're just starting and struggling to balance a day job with family life and launching a business, the secret is focus. Building a stable business takes time and effort, and it's easy to come home after a full day at work and just think, "I'm going to put my feet up." Instead, you need to be strict with yourself and treat it like a job. Decide how much time you will dedicate to your business each day, even if it's only an hour or two. Set yourself a time to start work and stop, block out those hours in your schedule every evening, and tell your family not to disturb you.

Simply setting the time aside isn't enough, however. Raj quickly discovered that if he just sat down at the computer without a plan, he'd start going through emails, browse the web, maybe tinker with a logo or a banner, and two hours later, he'd realize it was time to stop, but he hadn't made any progress.

What was missing was discipline. Now, when Raj sits down to work, he starts by making a list of exactly what he intends to achieve in the time. Knowing what he needs to get done allows him to focus during his working hours and be far more productive. And like others you've read about in this book, if he's working on a major task, like launching a product, he'll break it down into smaller steps that can be completed in the time available.

When you do this for yourself, you'll initially find it's still easy to get distracted, but after a while, you get into a rhythm. It's gratifying to stop at the end of the day knowing everything you've done to move towards your goal. It also makes it much easier to justify to your partner why they had to leave you alone!

It's equally important, however, to be disciplined about stopping work. At the end of your time slot, turn off the computer and go and enjoy some down time. Again, that's easier when you can point to a list of what you've accomplished, which is why Raj is such a fan of starting each work burst with a task list.

The important thing (and again, you'll read this from several of the entrepreneurs in this book) is to give yourself time off. If you don't, there's a risk that either you'll get burned out or you'll get resentful. And whether you resent the business for dragging you away from your family and friends, or you resent your family and friends for getting in the way of building your business, it's not a good thing either way! Remember: the whole point of building a business is not just to have more money but to enjoy a better lifestyle.

> *I'm a member of Nick James's coaching program. I wasn't new to info publishing when I joined (I'd already launched a few products), but I knew there were things I'd missed, and I was looking for new strategies to help scale the business.*

On one of our private coaching calls, we focused on pricing (an area I've struggled with in the past). PLR tends to be a low-ticket industry, and I'd priced my products at the bottom of the market. Nick helped me identify specific offers, like a membership program, that I could charge much more for. Then he helped him develop strategies to attract the right JV partners to promote those higher-ticket offers to the right audiences. **Raj Sidhu**

The Importance of a Coach

Raj is a great believer in the power of coaching, whatever stage you are at in building your business, and he sees two main reasons to use a coach. The first, of course, is to get accountability: you know that if you tell your coach you'll do something, they will ask whether you did it the next time you speak to them.

The second is that it gives you someone you can ask for advice when you hit a roadblock - and that's something you can only get from someone who is ahead of you in your business journey and has already faced and overcome the kind of challenge you're facing. Without that 'inside track,' it's too easy to waste days, weeks, or even months trying to find the answer for yourself.

Anyone who is thinking about getting into this industry should get to know Nick James. I've known him for a long time as a great mentor who is both successful in the industry and trustworthy. He has helped me with strategies specific to my business, and my sales have grown as a direct result. **Raj Sidhu**

Challenges

One of the biggest challenges Raj faced getting started was finding the business model for him. It's easy to get distracted in the online world because there are so many possible ways to go: affiliate marketing, Amazon FBA, building an agency, e-commerce, and more appearing every day.

The key, again, is focus. Many marketers choose a business model, try it for a couple of months and then give up because it's not working as quickly as they'd like. Raj's advice is to pick a model and stick with it. All the models can work, but it's your job to make one model work and only then expand into another.

Raj sees himself as a product creator rather than a teacher.

Once he'd finally found the PLR space, the next challenge Raj faced was productivity. When he was creating info products, he typically released something every six months. In the PLR industry, he can release a new product every six to eight weeks, and he doesn't have to worry about whether his audience will get tired - unlike consumers of information, resellers are always hungry for more. He can be working on two PLR launches at a time and already thinking ahead to the next. But to get to that level of multitasking, Raj had to master his workflow. So, he looked at each process involved in creating and launching a new product and asked a single question: How do I make this more efficient?

Tracking Success

Tracking your stats each time you release a product is critical. With every new launch, Raj aims to better the previous one, and the way to do that has been to go back each time and analyze how things went: How did this launch perform compared to the last? What worked, what didn't, and what could be done better? What could he add to the funnel? What new JV partners could he get on board?

The primary success metric, of course, is revenue: how much money did you make? But that's not the only number you need to track. Traffic - the number of viewers who come to your sales page - is an important indicator of the health of your business. It's a simple equation: the more people see your offer, the more money you'll make.

Linked to that is conversion: the percentage of those visitors who bought. If you only look at traffic and revenue, it's easy to think you're getting better even when conversion is dropping. Imagine that, on your first launch, you send 1,000 visitors to your page and make 200 sales. Then on the next, you get 2,000 visitors and make 300 sales.

On the face of it, you got more traffic, and you made more sales. But look at conversion: on the first launch, 20% (200/1,000) of visitors bought; on the second, it was only 15% (300/2,000). If that trend continues, you'll be in trouble. You'll need to drive more traffic every time just to keep sales level.

Poor conversion rates also make it harder to attract good JV partners. If a partner sends traffic to your offer and it converts poorly, they won't make as much money as they expected. Worse, JV and affiliate marketers know they'll lose a percentage of their subscribers each time they promote an offer to their list - it's known as "Attrition."

The more attractive and relevant an offer is for their list, the lower that attrition rate will be and the higher the conversion rate. Conversely, if conversion is low, it means the offer isn't attractive or relevant enough, and the attrition rate will be higher. So, not only will your partner make less money, but they'll also have burned more of their list in the process.

If you want a healthy business that makes you attractive to potential JV partners and affiliates, you need to focus on conversion, not total revenue. It's good for your business, anyway: the higher your conversion percentage is, the more money you'll make from each visitor.

Another important statistic to track alongside conversion is repeat purchases. If people buy one product from you and never come back, there's something wrong with your products. Conversely, once you get a reputation for releasing good products, it's easy to get repeat buyers, and Raj has built a base of regular customers who buy everything he releases.

Finally, you need to track the size of your list and the rate at which it's growing. Your list will be your primary source of traffic. Without a list of your own, you will always be dependent on JVs and paid traffic for your sales. That's a dangerous position to be in: if you lose a major partner, it could crush your business. And if paid ad costs rise (as they did in

2020 and again in 2022), it'll eat away your profits. That's why, as you've read in other chapters, a list of your own - one you control and can sell to whenever you want - is the most valuable asset you can have.

However, it doesn't have to be a huge list: you don't need tens of thousands of email addresses. Raj has done all of this with a relatively small list. In fact, he'd go as far as to say that the size of your list is nowhere near as important as how responsive that list is. At one time, Raj had a list of 5,000 names, but they weren't engaged and didn't buy. These days, his list is smaller, but they are much more responsive, and they buy his products.

Final Advice If You're on The Fence

To sum up what Raj says above, if you're considering starting an info publishing business, you need to be dedicated to this. It's a business, not a hobby. You also need to be passionate about what you're doing. Otherwise, it will be hard to keep working at it consistently over time.

Next, commit to a business model. You can't dabble at something for a few weeks and then switch. Every one of the business models you've seen in this book works - you're reading about them from people who've had success with them - but it's up to you to make them work *for you*.

Finally, like all the info publishers in this book, Raj says you need a coach and mentor: someone who has already built a successful career in this industry, and who will be able to guide you through any big blocks or challenges you hit. Otherwise, you'll either waste a lot of time trying to figure things out on your own or simply quit in despair and frustration. As others have said in this book, the easiest way to set yourself up for success is to find someone who's done what you're trying to do and model them.

CHAPTER 12

Paul Hollins

If you're a subscriber to my Internet Marketing Newsletter service, you probably already know Paul Hollins - he interviews all my guest experts. A radio presenter by profession, he has found multiple ways to monetize his experience and even bought out a seven-figure competitor at zero cost. Intrigued? Read on to find out how he did it.

Paul started as a presenter on local radio in the UK in the 1990s, and it didn't take him long to figure out the biggest downside to that industry: presenters are contractors, not employees. So, they don't get benefits like health insurance, paid sick leave, or a company pension, and they have zero job security. If a station owner decides their face (or their voice) doesn't fit, they're gone.

Paul didn't like that lack of security in broadcasting. He wanted something in place so that, if he ever found himself out of work, there would still be money coming in to pay the rent and bills. That "Plan B" was info publishing. Today, Paul runs successful companies on both sides of the Atlantic, licensing pre-recorded content to radio stations worldwide. In a way, you could think of it as PLR for the entertainment industry!

Becoming A Content Creator

Paul's first foray into content creation came when the station he was working for asked him to produce a weekly three-hour chart rundown show with one of the best-known radio DJs in the UK at the time, David "Kid" Jensen. Jensen had been one of the most popular presenters on the main national pop radio station before being headhunted by the UK's largest local radio network. He was a major radio celebrity and one of the network's most bankable assets.

Local stations typically can't afford to hire a big celebrity like Kid Jensen to front a show, and that gave Paul an idea: if several stations shared the production costs and Jensen's fee, they could all get the show at a fraction of the actual cost - a bit like fractional ownership of a private jet.

Paul asked for permission to license the show to local stations in other regions. In exchange, as more stations signed up, he'd reduce his fee for producing the show, and if he got enough interest, all the costs would be covered by those other networks. As it happened, he got more than enough customers, not only in the UK but overseas, too. The station bosses were happy because they were getting their headline show for free, and Paul was happy because he was getting paid a lot more in total by the other stations.

In the early days, the show was put together on a PC. This was before MP3 or other compressed audio formats, so every track was recorded in real time, then the 3-hour show was burned onto multiple CDs and mailed on a Thursday to (hopefully) arrive on Friday, ready for broadcast at the weekend. And there were many occasions when Paul would get a panicked phone call on a Friday evening from a producer asking where the disks were. When that happened, Paul or one of his team would have to spend Saturday driving around the country hand-delivering that week's show.

Over time, producing that three-hour show became a full-time job, which wasn't scalable (or even sustainable). Fortunately, technology has moved on, and these days, production of Paul's shows is automated. The host records their segments, and software inserts the tracks. The CDs (and anxiety) are also gone; instead, everything is delivered online. In fact, Paul's company, Blue Revolution, was the first radio production company in the world to deliver content over the internet.

The Day It All Nearly Went Away

As I said earlier, a challenge for radio presenters and producers is that they're contractors, not employees. That became very clear when Paul got a call from the station telling him they were going in a different direction and dropping the Kid Jensen show.

If Paul had been producing the show just for them, it would have been a disaster. Luckily, that wasn't the case: he had many other customers for it. Of course, he still had two major problems: Jensen's contract was with the station, and the show had been recorded in the network's studios.

Paul quickly got in touch with Jensen's agent and asked if his client would be interested in continuing to host the show independently. He agreed, and a quick negotiation set the fee for future episodes. Fortunately, the agent also had a makeshift sound studio in his home that the team could use while they searched for a more permanent solution.

Getting Into Info Publishing

Over the years, Paul has grown his 'stable' of presenters, adding 80s pop legend Kim Wilde, Def Leppard's Joe Elliott, and many others. However, that's not what has driven growth. The key to making the business work was that Paul treated it as an online info publishing business right from the start.

Paul's first website was a *.co.uk* domain - he only bought a .com after the company won a major international radio award and started getting inquiries from around the world. Like many new entrepreneurs, when he set up the business, Paul expected customers to come flooding to his new website. However, he quickly discovered that's not how online business works: you have to drive traffic if you want to make sales.

So, Paul started looking for ways to promote the business beyond simply mailing letters and flyers to cold prospects. He had seen ads for online marketing events in the UK and signed up for one run by Frank Garon, who had flown across from the US to present in London.

"It was a typical hypey event like you got back in 2000: lots of speakers telling you that you could become a millionaire in your underwear. However, one speaker stood out because he was teaching the 'how to,' not just promising to teach you if you paid him. That was Nick James. He was talking about creating audio products, which immediately appealed to me, but also, there was no hyperbole: it was just good, honest advice.

All the presenters had been talking about the importance of growing a list and setting up autoresponders, but they hadn't said how to do it. So, I still didn't even know how to get started. After his talk, I asked Nick how to get subscribers, and he said I needed to offer something of value in exchange for their contact details. He suggested I offer a newsletter or a weekly tips sheet and put a sign-up form on our home page." **Paul Hollins**

Back then, everyone was talking about ezines, so Paul launched the Blue Revolution Ezine. Rather than try to do it himself, he invited other radio industry consultants to write articles for it, and he paid a graphic designer to put it all together.

Subscriptions quickly snowballed. It started with just ten subscribers, then 100, and 400. People were sharing it with colleagues inside their stations and in other networks, and the sign-ups kept coming.

That ezine and the .com domain - which he paid $5,000 for because someone else had already registered it before him - were some of the best investments Paul has made in his business.

Becoming Competition-Proof

The biggest struggle is the need to be constantly innovating and to stay top of mind. By his own admission, Paul doesn't email his list as often as he should, but it hasn't stopped him from making money as an info publisher, and the company does make extensive use of social media in its marketing.

As technology has moved forward - to the point where everyone has access to pro-grade equipment, and anyone can publish content online at the touch of a button - barriers to entry in Paul's industry have come down one by one.

Fortunately, Blue Revolution has one major factor to protect it: its reputation. The company has a track record for reliability, timeliness, and quality and for the status of the celebrities they attract to host their shows. You can probably see how that became a virtuous circle: you don't get one without the other. And it means that, as new competitors have tried to come into the market, Paul was able to stand up to them.

I can't stress enough how important your brand will be in your own business: if you can get known for producing high-quality content and excellent customer service, you'll be able to protect yourself from new competitors much more easily.

For the celebrities, there's a simple appeal to this business model: pop stars live from new release to new release (just like many info publishers!) and from tour to tour. In between, they need ways to stay in touch with their fans. Hosting a show gets them in front of their audience every week, and listeners can keep up on what's been going on in their idol's life and what's coming up next.

Think about how you could apply this to your own business. First, how can you help other business owners to get in front of their audience regularly, and how could you monetize that? Could you turn it into a service as Paul has? Or could they make an offer during those appearances and pay you as an affiliate?

Second, are there other business owners who can put you in front of their audience? That could be on a podcast, on their stage (live or virtual) or a webinar, in their newsletter, or whatever. And how could you make that worth their while: would you pay them an affiliate commission on the sales you make or a one-off fee for bringing you on? Or perhaps you could do a swap and promote each other free to your respective lists.

Finding The Next Product Idea

Paul's second product was aimed at presenters rather than radio stations. And because Paul is a working radio presenter, he knows that market and their needs very well.

DJs have to prepare for their show: finding out what's in the news, what's happening locally, the latest celebrity gossip, what's happening in the charts, and lining up trivia and jokes to entertain their audience. That means they have to buy all the national and local papers, trawl a bunch of websites, scroll through the TV schedules, etc. For a breakfast show presenter who is probably having to get up at 3 a.m., taking that chore off their to-do list would mean they get another 30 minutes or an hour in bed, and for a daytime or evening DJ, that's time they can spend with their family, or earning money doing voiceovers.

So, Paul realized there was value in a service that did that research on a daily basis. He spoke to a fellow presenter (who was already doing research for his own show) and made him an irresistible offer: "Just do what you're currently doing for free, let me sell it to other radio presenters, and I'll give you 33% of the revenue. You don't need to do anything different or new."

There's a critical point in this: Paul doesn't do the research himself. Instead, he found someone who was already doing the work and offered to pay him for it. Paul's job as a business owner is not the "doing" of the work; it's the marketing. You can apply the same principle in your business to create a product in any niche, even if you don't have the necessary skills. Simply find someone with valuable knowledge and figure out how to get others to pay for it.

> *People around me kept saying, "You could create the content yourself and keep 100% of the money. Why are you paying someone else to do it?" Nick James was one of the only people who challenged that. He said, "Why would you create a job for yourself where you have to get up every morning at 3 a.m. - whether you feel like it or not - and churn out new content constantly? Why would you do that to yourself when you've already found someone who's happy to do it for you?"* **Paul Hollins**

By now, you're probably thinking, "But why wouldn't that person just sell it themselves and cut Paul out of the equation?" Simple: If they knew marketing and sales, they'd already be doing it. Or perhaps they know how, but they don't want to have to do it. Either way, it's easier for them to partner with someone who has marketing and sales skills and enjoys that kind of thing.

That's how Paul's "Prep Sheet" business was born. Subscribers got an email every day at 5.30 a.m. with everything they needed for that day. And to make it a no-brainer, Paul looked at what a presenter would typically spend on newspapers - about £100 each month ($150 at the time) - and set the subscription at £39 ($60), so the presenters weren't just getting back time, they were also saving money.

> *There may be stuff someone else is already doing that you can package up and publish: as the publisher, you collect the revenues and pay the creator a fair fee. It's a triple win. The writer gets paid, you get paid, and the customers enjoy the benefit of whatever it is you're creating. Just remember that you deserve to be paid for coming up with a way to monetize it and for running the business.* **Paul Hollins**

And to make it even easier to become a customer, Paul offered a seven-day trial for just £1 ($1.50). Why not free? First, it meant he collected payment details right at the start, so he could charge at the end of the trial without having to ask for any more information. Second, it made the revenue in a customer's first month £40 instead of £39. That may not sound like much of a difference, but when thousands of people are paying it, those $1.50's quickly add up.

The key to making the business work was to automate as much of the process as possible - the writer would log on each morning and upload that day's pdf, then the system attached it to a broadcast email that went out to all active subscribers. Payment was automated via PayPal, and if someone canceled their subscription, the system moved them out of the active list (so they stopped getting the daily delivery email) into a reactivation sequence where they received a series of offers designed to encourage them back. That's a smart move, and it brought back around 15% of that 'lost' business.

Paul also noticed that the rate of unsubscribes was highest after four months. So, he added an email series in month three that teased additional subscriber benefits coming up in future months.

That extra tweak added another six months to the average customer lifetime: that's an extra £240 ($360) of revenue from each subscriber just for doing some quick analytics on retention and attrition rates - and at the time, Paul had over a thousand subscribers.

Getting Bought Out

Paul wasn't the only person in this line of business - there was a competitor who had been around longer and noticed that sales were falling. Rather than take Paul on head-to-head, he decided it would be easier to buy him out. So, he came to Paul with a simple question: "How much do you want for the business?" (i.e., *What will it cost me to make you go away?*)

The answer was a multiple of the average annual profits. The competitor paid, and Paul was free to move on to other business ideas, but with a substantial reserve of money to reinvest. Paul also made sure that his writer was taken care of - he went with the business and carried on creating content for the new owner. And over time, the writer has made enough money to buy a holiday home in Florida, doing something he was going to do anyway.

Now think about this: if it had been Paul who was creating the content, it would have been much harder to sell the business (unless he wanted to become the new owner's employee), or the value would have been substantially lower (because he'd only be selling a customer list). It's a trap many entrepreneurs have fallen into. But by having a 'real' business, with other people doing the work, Paul had created something that someone could take over and run without him

In business, you'll constantly face a choice: "Do I want to continue to grow this business, or should I cash out and move on to the next thing?" Follow your head and the numbers rather than letting your heart lead, even though it can be quite an emotional decision. After all, you'll have spent a few years growing your "baby" to where it is, and it must be doing well. Otherwise, no one would be interested in buying it. But could you use the energy and money you'll be freeing up to do something even bigger and better?

Name Dropping for Fun and Profit

Over the years, Paul has talked to many top stars, whether as a presenter or for his production business, and every time he got someone on the line, he would ask them to record a quick "Hi, I'm Madonna" or "Hi, I'm Billy Joel" or whoever they were. They're known in the industry as "artist drops," and they're an easy sale because stations love to insert them at the start of an ad for the channel. And the great thing is it doesn't take any extra work to create that product: the celebrity is already speaking to Paul, so all he has to do is ask them to say "Hello."

Paul has many volumes of these recordings - 850 stars in total collected over 15 years - which he sells online: a producer visits the site, decides which volume or volumes they want to buy (or they can bundle all volumes together at a discounted price), and enters their credit card details. And, of course, it's all automated, so the money comes in with minimal effort on Paul's part.

And celebrities aren't the only people radio stations want to hear from. Over the years, producers would ask Paul if he had recordings of "normal" people saying things like, "You guys play the best music." Or "This is my favorite station." Paul didn't have anything like that, and he knew it would take time to create - it meant taking a team out onto the streets to record passersby and then lots of editing to make everything sound clean.

However, he knew someone who had lost her job at a radio station and had started recording friends, family, and neighbors saying these short phrases. She had collected over 1,000 clips and turned them into a product called Listener Vault. The problem was that she didn't have the marketing skills she needed, so she'd only been able to make a handful of sales.

Paul watched as she dropped her price from $89 to $69, and finally, to $49. He reached out, told her he loved what she had done, and asked what her plans were for the product. She admitted that she'd just taken a job at a station and didn't have any time to keep working on the product.

Paul sensed an opportunity and asked whether he could buy it from her. She said yes, and Blue Revolution had another product for its library. And because she'd only made a handful of sales, the product creator only wanted $1,225 for her business.

So, Paul only needed to sell 25 copies at $49 to his list of 15,000 radio stations, which he knew was very doable - the product was an excellent match for anyone who had bought artist drops over the years. Not all of them would buy, of course, but there was a good chance that a significant proportion would, especially at such a low price. It was also the perfect "order bump" to offer anytime someone bought an artist drop library (just like the server at McDonald's asking, "Do you want fries with that?").

> *The seller was happy because she finally made some money from her work. She's looking forward to seeing how we grow her "baby," and she loved the negotiation process so much that she's talking about doing more work with us on an ongoing basis. She's already started working on a Christmas edition for us!* **Paul Hollins**

There are several lessons here that you can take into your own business. A big one is that if you find someone who is struggling to monetize a product, they'll often be willing to sell or license it to you very cheaply just so they can finally make some money from it. Then you can apply your marketing skills to turn the potential of that product into a profitable reality, especially if you have a list of proven buyers ready and waiting for it. In the end, a buyer is a buyer: once you've built a list of customers, keep looking for new products and services you can offer them and new ways to monetize that list.

How To Buy Your Competitor and Get Them to Pay For It

Back in the 1990s, the radio station Paul was working for sent him to California to work with a production company called Radio Express. They created shows with celebrity hosts and licensed them to local stations across the US - in fact, it was the owner of Radio Express, Tom Rounds, who suggested to Paul that he could copy the model in the UK market.

Over the years, Tom became a mentor to Paul, and when he died, Paul contacted his widow to offer his condolences and told her that if she ever wanted to sell the business, he'd be interested. That day came in 2018, and Paul negotiated what is known as a 'seller-financed' buyout: He and the seller agreed on a price for the business, and he made an initial deposit (which he put on the company credit card). The rest of the money was to be paid over three years.

From Tom's widow's perspective, it gave her a lump sum up front and a guaranteed income for the next three years, so she was happy. From Paul's point of view, it was also a great deal. On the face of it, Blue Revolution and Radio Express were competitors. However, Blue Revolution focused on the UK, Europe, the Middle East, Australia, and New Zealand, while Radio Express served the US and Africa. So, the deal gave Paul almost global coverage with minimal overlap.

And because Radio Express wasn't a struggling startup, there wasn't much risk. On the contrary, the company was well-established in its industry, with a team and a loyal customer base. Even more importantly, it was profitable and generating positive cash flow, so Paul knew the payments would be covered. And he also saw that there would be opportunities for both companies to cross-sell content to the other's customers and areas where he could save money by sharing resources and expenses between Radio Express and Blue Revolution.

A great example of this is server costs. Blue Revolution was paying €250 per year (about $325) for server space, while Radio Express was paying $900 every month. By switching suppliers, Paul saved over $10,000 per year. The company was also paying $100 every month for a cable subscription for a TV in the break room that no one watched. Paul suggested that as a production company, it would be nice to play their own shows or stream their clients' stations. Another $7,000 saving came from canceling old domain names the company wasn't using but had kept renewing.

Little by little, the savings added up, a few hundred dollars here, a thousand dollars there, until Paul had added $70,000 a year to the bottom line, which over three years was enough to pay for the buyout! Paul effectively bought the company for free by being able to rationalize and be more efficient. And this was a company with a seven-figure turnover and mid-six-figure profits.

> *"I love startups, and I've created a few over the years, but it can be great for your business to buy an established competitor if there are synergies that will save you money, they have assets you can use in both companies, or they're driving traffic that would also be valuable in your business. Or you can think of it as simply buying their list, knowing it's full of proven buyers you can market to. Either way, I'd rather spend my money on that than on marketing to cold prospects."*
> **Paul Hollins**

You might think that running a global production business working with lots of high-profile celebrities means Paul needs huge teams. In fact, he only has a handful of people in the US, another two or three in the UK, and two in Europe. And since 2020, everyone has worked remotely, so there are no premises costs, which has increased profitability even more.

"Revenue Bumps"

One of the big advantages of running an info publishing business is most noticeable when you need cash in a hurry. For an employee, there are very few options: they can go to the bank and (as long as they're not already in debt) they might get a loan, they can beg their boss for a raise, or if they're lucky, they can ask a family member to help. For an info publisher, there's a much more straightforward solution: what marketing legend Bill Glazer calls "sending the bill to your list."

Over the years since attending his first marketing conference, Paul has created several products outside the radio niche. One of the first was a simple ebook called The Zero Cost Method.

Paul was at one of my events, and he noticed that in the breaks, people were coming up with all sorts of reasons why they couldn't implement what they were learning. One of the most frequent excuses was cost: "I can't afford $20 a month for an autoresponder and $100 for webinar software."

On his way home, Paul started thinking about how he could show people that it's not that expensive to run an info-publishing business (of course, if you've read this far in this book, you already know it doesn't cost much to get started or to get going!). So, he created a 37-page PDF listing free software for managing emails, running webinars, building a website, finding stock images, and everything else a new publisher might need. It was information anyone could have found for free in a few hours on Google. But, he priced it at £10 ($15), and within 48 hours of launching it, he'd made $4,500 in sales. (I actually told him he should sell it for at least $47 and that he needed a back end!). Then he brought on some affiliates, and sales really took off.

Now he had a list of proven buyers in the info publishing and internet marketing niche. So, for his next product, Paul turned to a site that's very popular in those industries: Fiverr.com. He'd been outsourcing a lot of graphic design work to people on the site, and he noticed that sellers were offering to edit audio files, but no one was offering audio processing.

Podcasting was taking off, and Paul knew from his work in radio that one of the biggest headaches for interviewers is when people's mics are set to different levels, so one person is very loud while another can barely be heard. He asked around and confirmed that the same thing happened to podcasters, and they'd have to spend a few hours editing an interview - boosting one person and bringing down the volume of the other - to try to get something usable.

Paul had expensive professional-grade software he used in his production business to correct that problem. All he had to do was drop in an audio file, and a few seconds later, out popped a clean, perfectly balanced recording.

He set himself up on Fiverr and got a flurry of orders. Then he created a second gig offering to remove background noise and hiss, eliminate pops and clicks, and all the other little annoyances that plague anyone who has ever recorded audio outside a professional studio. Again, he was using software that he was already paying for, and the key was that these were subscription-based programs, and most content creators don't want to pay subscriptions for things they're not using all the time.

Paul was making $40 or $50 a day (about $1,000 a month) for around 30 minutes of work. So, he spent a day and a half researching and writing a $17 report called The Fiverr Formula to teach others how to do something similar with whatever skills and software they had available.

For the launch, Paul brought on affiliates (including me) and bundled together both products (The Fiverr Formula and the Zero Cost Method). The top affiliate generated $10,000 in sales in just 8 minutes (but that's a story for another time!).

Then I suggested Paul turn the PDF into an audio product. So, he recorded himself reading the PDF, put it onto an MP3 player, priced it at $75, recruited affiliates, and made 1,000 sales. That's $75,000 in sales of a product that was basically Paul reading his $17 ebook. Why would people buy that? Because some people would rather listen to audio than read a PDF, and they're willing to pay for that.

Here's the twist: Paul is still making sales of both products every day, but he's so busy running his radio production businesses that he doesn't have time to do anything more with them. So, what can he do to monetize them further? He has decided to license the content to other info publishers who can promote the product to their lists and keep 100% of the profits. Unlike when he sold the Prep Sheet business, however, the licenses for this are non-exclusive, so he can sell multiple licenses. Licensing a proven product to other marketers is a great way to cash in when you decide to move your attention to new projects.

"I believe that in internet marketing, everybody's voice is unique. Anyody can put together an audio product or write a book - but you have to commit. If you commit and take it out into the market, good things will happen. Most people get 95% of the way there, but they stop because they're afraid. 'What if it flops? Or what if it's really successful and it takes over my life?"

"Well, maybe it will flop. Or maybe it will take off and overwhelm you. But maybe it will be a great success that brings you a chunk of additional money for work you've already done. You'll never find out, unless you take the chance." **Paul Hollins**

Conclusion

In this book, I have done my best to show you - warts and all - what it's like to be an info publisher. You've seen people who started their business in their 20s, and others who started after they retired; people who launched themselves into a completely new career or turned a hobby into a business, and others who took the work they were doing as an employee and simply fired their boss.

This is about a completely different way of making money, where you're not stuck trading time for money. You can build a business around any skill or information you have (or can learn) and do it on your own terms. You can build it alongside your main career, or it can be your main career. You can do it full-time or part-time. You can use it to pay your bills or to buy luxuries. And sometimes - as you saw in Amber's story - you may start a business to supplement your family's income and it becomes your family's main source of income. You could even end up being your significant other's boss!

Those choices are all down to you. But they are available to you because you're an info publisher - 90% of people don't enjoy that freedom because they're stuck in a 9-5 job. And the flexibility of this career is endless. If you love to be on camera, there's a way you can do it. If you have "a face for radio", there's a path for you too. And if you just love to write, this career is perfect for you too.

Whatever your life has been like up to this point, you can draw a line under it and get a fresh start. It doesn't matter whether you've enjoyed huge professional success or endured years of struggle, whether you've achieved financial security or you're flat broke, whether you're young or old, married, single, or "it's complicated": all you need is a desire to help others achieve a goal, and the ability to provide that help in whatever form you (and they) prefer.

The key is to stop looking for excuses not to get started. I remember reading an article by Dan Kennedy - one of the greatest copywriters in the world - where he pointed out that a lot of people misuse the word "can't" when they really mean "choose not to." For example, if you've been telling yourself "I can't afford to start an info publishing business," think about what that really means. In this book, you've seen that it doesn't take a huge investment to set up this sort of business; time is a far more important investment than money.

Which means that what you're really saying is, "I choose not to put my time into starting an info publishing business." Because everything you do - or don't do - in life is driven by the choices you make. So, if you're choosing not to put time and energy into starting your business, ask yourself where you're putting that time and energy instead.

And then ask yourself whether that's really a better use of your time and energy than starting a business.

Even if you're thinking, "But what about the cost of web hosting? I have to pay to put a website online!" Ask yourself whether you really can't afford a few dollars a month to secure your financial future. I'm pretty sure that if I looked at your credit card or bank statements for the last few months, I'd find a few things you chose to pay for rather than put that money into your business, whether it's a Netflix subscription, a couple of pints of beer, or hopping on the bus instead of walking to the shops.

The same goes for excuses like, "I can't start my business because I'm too old/too young." Why are you choosing to believe that there is some sort of age limit on starting a business? Is that limit real, or did you make it up?

It's time to look at the choices you're making and ask yourself whether you really want to start a business. Because, as Dan Kennedy points out in his article, when you don't want to do something, one excuse is just as good as another.

The people in this book chose to stop making excuses and start taking action instead., and they chose to share their story to help you and inspire you to make the same choices.

Of course, when you read a testimonial paragraph on a page or watch a 30-second testimonial video, the questions that inevitably come up in your mind are, "That's all well and good, but what did it really take to get there? Where did this person start, and what is their life really like now?"

That's why I asked each of the people in this book to share every detail: what they were doing before info publishing, why they chose to start, what it took, how much time and energy they had to put into it, the struggles they faced, the times they stumbled and had to pick themselves up, their failures as well as their successes. And I asked them to share what success means to them.

I wanted you to know what to expect - the good, the bad, and the life-changing.

I wanted you to know that there will be challenges and struggles along the way; times when you'll look at your business and wonder if it's ever going to be a success; when you'll question whether you made the right decision or a horrible mistake.

But, at the start of this book, I also promised you that **there is support available** to help you get started, overcome the challenges, and **achieve success on your own terms.**

So, I wanted to give you all the information **you need to make a decision about your future** and to **say yes to opportunity**.

This may be the first time you've come across the idea of info publishing, or you may have been thinking about it for a while, sitting on the sidelines, watching other people grow their own successful info publishing business and wondering when it will be your turn.

Well, **it's your turn.**

YOU are in control of the next step.

It's your choice.

The question is are you brave enough to **make the decision and take action** to get what you ultimately want? (And maybe end up sharing **your success** story in my next book!)

If you are, then I'd like to help you get there.

So, if you're ready to explore how to **start your info publishing business** - or if you're an info publisher looking to **grow the business you already have** - I'd like to invite you to **take the next step.**

To continue the journey, simply head over to

www.nick-james.com/nextsteps

It's Your Turn

If you're ready to explore how to start your info publishing business - or if you're an info publisher looking to grow the business you already have - I'd like to invite you to take the next step.

To continue the journey, simply head over to

www.nick-james.com/nextsteps

Printed in Great Britain
by Amazon